VISION, HONOR

PETER CHAR

AND MALE FRIENDSHıı

L'ENFANT

IN THE EARLY AMERICAN REPUBLIC

Kenneth R. Bowling

PRINTED FOR THE FRIENDS OF
THE GEORGE WASHINGTON UNIVERSITY LIBRARIES

Washington, D.C.
September 2002

♀ GW Graphic Design 60810   ISBN 0-9727611-0-1

To Myrtle Cheney Murdock

(1886–1980)

Columnist

Author

Champion of Constantino Brumidi

And United States Capitol Guide,

Who instilled in me a lifelong interest in the history of

Congress, the Capitol and Washington, D.C.

The 30th Anniversary of the Friends of the GW Libraries

This volume commemorates the 30th anniversary of the Friends of the University Libraries at The George Washington University. Much has changed since October 1, 1972, when the Friends published their first book, "A Woman in the Case: The Suppressed Commencement Address of 1887" by Elliott Coues, M.D. You now hold the 30th Anniversary volume, which also examines history, with even farther reach. Those who established the Friends group in 1972 saw both the Melvin Gelman Library as well as the Paul Himmelfarb Health Sciences Library groundbreaking in 1973. The Jacob Burns Law Library had been opened in 1967. Take a look around the GW libraries now. Along with improvements to the buildings and continuing efforts to enhance library collections, services and space, we have expanded "unbound" into the digital age. The GW libraries, members of the prestigious Association of Research Libraries, celebrated in 2001 the addition of the Two-millionth Volume to the collections. We extend our gratitude to members of the Friends of the GW Libraries and everyone who has helped build the GW library system up to its present capacity. By enhancing the libraries, we enhance our future.

Jack A. Siggins
University Librarian

Walter E. Beach
President, Friends of the GW Libraries

PREFACE

For years I was puzzled by why Pierre Charles L'Enfant had used the name Peter Charles L'Enfant when he purchased a Washington, D.C., lot at the October 1791 sale. When I decided to find out why, my initial research quickly established the fact that he stopped using the former name soon after coming to the United States. Why he did so became one aspect of a talk that I presented in April 2001 to the Friends of the University Libraries. I had realized by then, and particularly after additional research, that L'Enfant gave far more to the early American republic than just the design of Washington, D.C., for which he had been resurrected as a Frenchman and apotheosized in the early twentieth century. Thus this book, an effort to which many people have contributed.

My greatest debt is to three individuals whose interest in and knowledge of L'Enfant predated my own. All three read and commented on the manuscript. Phil Ogilvie of the Department of Tourism at The George Washington University saved me hours of work by loaning me his extensive research files on both L'Enfant and French Ambassador Jules Jusserand. Over the course of several years Pamela Scott and Donald Hawkins have shared their insights about L'Enfant.

My colleagues at the First Federal Congress Project, Charlene Bickford, Helen Veit, and William diGiacomantonio, put up with my bursts of enthusiasm and read and proofread the manuscript, which benefitted greatly from their efforts. In addition, diGiacomantonio researched and composed the captions for the illustrations and saw the book through the production stage. The Friends of the University Libraries, who have sponsored publication of this book, have graciously donated any profits from the sale of the book to the Project.

Librarians and archivists as always played a special role. At the National Archives Cynthia Fox, Robert Ellis, and Dane Hartgrove helped me with census and court records. At the Historical Society of Washington, D.C., Gail R. Redmann quickly and graciously answered several questions by telephone. The staff of the Manuscript Division of the Library of Congress patiently pulled whatever collection I thought might add a twist or a tidbit to the evolving story; in particular I am in debt to Mary Wolfskill, Jeff Flannery, Bruce R. Kirby, Patrick Kerwin, Ahmed Johnson, Ernie Emrich, and Fred Bauman. Ellen McCallister Clark guided me in the use of the wonderful research library of The Society of the Cincinnati. Several others assisted in my attempt to discover the meaning of William Temple Franklin's January 1787 letter to L'Enfant: Rob Cox and Whitfield J. Bell of the American Philosophical Society, James N. Green of the Library Company of Philadelphia, Mark Piel of the New York Society Library, and Coxie Toogood of Independence National Historical Park.

A variety of friends and scholars lent their expertise and/or editorial eye: Betty Nuxoll, C. M. Harris, Barbara Oberg, Barbara Wolanin, Cynthia Earman, Bob Arnebeck, Christopher Gray, John D. Gordan III, Gaspare J. Saladino, Richard Leffler, James M. Goode, Brian Lang, Jane Levey, Lenore D. Miller, Donald Kennon, Bruce Ragsdale, Mark Richards, Allida Black, John Allan Gable, Elizabeth A. Fenn, Richard H. and Lynne H. Kohn, Julie V. Curtis, William Alverson, and Roberta Spalter-Roth.

Erica Aungst of the Gelman Library mothered the book from its inception. Peter Hines and Amanda Davies of GW Graphic Design made the production process pleasant and expeditious; the book demonstrates Amanda's talents well.

French Ambassador Jules Jusserand, who wrote the first biography of L'Enfant, once noted that his subject was linguistically challenged in French as well as English. Reflecting that observation, I have modernized spelling and capitalization where I felt it necessary for clarity and ease of reading.

Kenneth R. Bowling
Washington, D.C.
July 2002

"We are only too proud and eager to say to every one visiting" Washington "that this is the plan of a Frenchman, who came to us in our need."[1] Thus did Glenn Brown, secretary of the American Institute of Architects, characterize the early twentieth century apotheosis of "Pierre" Charles L'Enfant as a Frenchman. This little book seeks to shed light on the personality and importance of Peter Charles L'Enfant (or P. Charles L'Enfant as he most often signed his name after 1790): the French-born American, who soon stopped using "Pierre" after his arrival in the United States in 1777, who was identified in federal records during his lifetime as Peter, and who enumerated himself in the 1820 census as a citizen of the United States.

At a congressional committee meeting in 1789, held in the wake of his triumphal creation of Federal Hall in New York City, L'Enfant was so loquacious "that scarce a word could be said" by anybody else.[2] He wrote like he spoke and consequently few Americans of his generation left posterity such lengthy, soul baring accounts of themselves. Perhaps his difficulties with the English language contributed to this. More likely it was a combination of his personality and his French heritage. An independent, creative visionary a century ahead of his time both as an engineer and a city planner, L'Enfant believed that his adopted country was destined to be a great commercial republic. He had the courage to plan and advocate for that vision of the future no matter the personal cost. His ideas and images impressed those in the revolutionary leadership who shared his commitment to a pro-active federal government. George Washington, Alexander Hamilton, Robert Morris, James Monroe, Henry Knox, and Frederick William Steuben in particular did what they could to further his career, even when L'Enfant's sense of honor and sensitivity to slight led him to goad and rebuke them. Thomas Jefferson, who also worked closely with the city planner for a brief but critical period, was less impressed by him and certainly found his vision for the United States repugnant. While Jefferson's view of America's future came to dominate the Early American Republic, that of L'Enfant and the others would prevail within a century.

Peter Charles L'Enfant was born in Paris on 2 August 1754 to Marie Charlotte Lullier Lenfant, the daughter of an official of the French Court, and Pierre Lenfant, a painter retained by the Court and associated with the Gobelins Tapestry Works. He was baptized into the Catholic faith the next day, grew up at the courts of Louis XV and XVI, and at seventeen became a student of his father at the Royal Academy of

Frederick William Steuben
Frederick William Augustus, Baron von Steuben (1730–94) was the most colorful character on Washington's military staff, and a devoted patron and father figure for several young Continental Army officers. L'Enfant, who was one of them, executed eight illustrations for Steuben's famous military manual in 1779. This painting by Charles Willson Peale (1741–1827) shows the flamboyant Prussian volunteer in an array of foreign decorations a year or two before he would have donned the badge of The Society of the Cincinnati, which he helped establish in 1783. In 1789 he was the only non-government official present on the balcony of Federal Hall during Washington's inauguration. A year later, after petitioning Congress for eight years, Steuben finally received an annuity as compensation for his wartime service. (Courtesy of Independence National Historical Park, Philadelphia)

Alexander Hamilton
Alexander Hamilton (1755–1804) became one of L'Enfant's first and most important bonds to his adopted country while serving as a lieutenant colonel and Washington's long time aide de camp during the Revolutionary War. In the quarter century-long friendship that ensued, Hamilton aided L'Enfant—promoting his petitions and lining up important commissions—as a congressman during the Confederation, "boss" of New York City's Federalist political machine, principal advisor to the directors of the Society for Establishing Useful Manufactures, and first secretary of the treasury (1789–95). This portrait was executed by John Trumbull (1756–1843) two years after Hamilton's death. (Courtesy of the National Portrait Gallery, Smithsonian Institution, Washington, D.C.)

Painting and Sculpture where he studied architecture and drawing. He must not have found the life of a student satisfying, for at the age of twenty-two, he accepted a lieutenancy in the Continental Army offered him by Silas Deane, the American secret agent at Paris.[3] Thus he became part of the wave of French aristocrats seeking glory by crossing the Atlantic to have another crack at John Bull by supporting the American cause. In 1777, when L'Enfant arrived in the United States, it is likely that he planned to return to France at the end of the festivities. But this was not to be the course of his difficult life, and by the end of the Revolutionary War he had anglicized his name and committed his talents to enhancing the "glory and interest of these United States."[4] For his contribution to American patriotic iconography, for his design of Washington, D.C., and in particular for his vision of America's destiny, Peter Charles L'Enfant merits a more important place in early American history.

"SECURING TO THE UNITED STATES A PEACEFUL AND TRANQUIL ENJOYMENT OF LIBERTY"

The engineer Tronson de Coudray reported to the Continental Congress that L'Enfant had talent for drawing, but nothing useful for engineering except "embellishing plans with cartouches." This may have contributed to its decision to send him to Boston early in 1778 to assist the Prussian army veteran Frederich William von Steuben, who left Europe for America in part to escape a smear campaign headed by the local Catholic clergy, that included allegations that he had "taken familiarities" with boys. Benjamin Franklin had lavishly exaggerated Steuben's military rank in recommending him to Congress; the hyperbole proved to be fortunate, for his contribution to the success of the War for Independence was matched by few. At Boston, as Steuben's secretary and interpreter, the bright seventeen year old aristocrat Peter Stephen DuPonceau recalled years later, L'Enfant found Steuben, his French aides, his young German servant Carl, and his large spoiled Italian dog Azor, none of whom (other than DuPonceau) could speak a word of English—although Azor had a good ear for music. L'Enfant escorted Steuben and his suite to York, Pennsylvania, where Congress sat during its exile from British-occupied Philadelphia. At Steuben's insistence Congress promoted L'Enfant to captain of engineers in the Continental Army. From there the entourage ventured east to Valley Forge where L'Enfant met George Washington (of whom he drew a pencil portrait), Henry Knox and James Monroe, all of whom would play important roles in his life. Most importantly, he came to know Alexander Hamilton and John Laurens, who were appointed by Washington to assist Steuben, in part because of their command of French.[5]

With the assistance of DuPonceau, Hamilton, Laurens and Benjamin Walker, Steuben immediately set about preparing his *Regulations, Orders, and Discipline for the Army of the United States*, which remained the official military manual of the United States Army until after the War of 1812. L'Enfant did eight illustrations for it and received a bonus of $500 from Congress. In April 1779, seeing no opportunity for the glory of an active military campaign in the North, L'Enfant traveled to Charleston, South Carolina, where his friend Laurens offered him command of the corps of slaves he planned to raise. When political opposition proved too strong for Laurens to succeed in what he openly avowed was part of his commitment to abolishing slavery, L'Enfant remained with the engineer corps.

He soon regretted his decision to come South, complaining to Steuben about both his superiors and his rank. Nevertheless, his valor while attempting to set fire to the British abatis during the Franco-American siege of Savannah, Georgia, in October 1779 earned him the lifelong respect of the Continental Army officer corps as well as a serious leg wound. Originally presumed dead on the battlefield, L'Enfant was rescued and taken to Charleston where he remained bedridden until January.[6] He may have relied on a cane (though this may have been an affectation like the apostrophe that he added to his surname) as well as alcohol and even opiates as pain relievers for the rest of his life. Still on one crutch, L'Enfant participated in the ill-fated defense of Charleston in May 1780 and was taken prisoner by the British. He was paroled after a brief but traumatic imprisonment.[7] Parole meant that he could perform no military service for the United States and confined him to nearby Christ Church Parish; the latter restriction was removed in July 1781 and he apparently went to Philadelphia. Nineteen months after his capture, an exchange of prisoners in January 1782 finally allowed L'Enfant to return to active military duty. Laurens renewed his offer of a commission with the rank of major in the slave corps he still hoped to raise, but L'Enfant decided that, even given the promotion to which he so adamantly thought himself entitled, greater advantage would come from remaining with the engineers. An appeal to Washington for intervention on behalf of a rank increase to major elicited personal praise from the commander in chief but no majority from Congress.[8]

L'Enfant's career changed dramatically in April 1782 when Washington honored a request from the French Ambassador that the engineer build a hall at Philadelphia for a celebration of the birth of the French Dauphin (later Louis XVII). L'Enfant designed a lavishly decorated sixty by forty foot building that for the first time displayed his genius for patriotic iconography. Eleven hundred people attended the costly and diplomatically important 15 July event—until then probably the largest, most extravagant and memorable party ever held north of Mexico. It brought together many of the leaders of the Revolution from its early pamphlet protests of the 1760s through the congressional and military battlefields of the 1770s and 1780s: "Pennsylvania Farmer" John Dickinson could be seen conversing one moment with George Washington and another with

Signature on Receipt
This is a receipt for contributions collected from New Jersey and New Hampshire officers for L'Enfant's purchase of Society of the Cincinnati diplomas. Dated West Point, New York, 15 October 1783, it is the earliest known document in which L'Enfant signs his name "Peter," although undoubtedly he had anglicized his name earlier. The document also establishes a possible date for his grand painting of West Point that appears on the back cover of this book. (From the collection of The Society of the Cincinnati Archives, Washington, D.C.)

Superintendent of Finance Robert Morris, the elegantly appointed Count Rochambeau spent time with an Indian ally in native dress, and Thomas Paine kept stepping away from the crowd "to analyze his thoughts and to enjoy the repast of his own original ideas."[9]

Perhaps the party helped L'Enfant gain his long-sought majority, recommended in May 1783 by a congressional committee that included his former comrade Alexander Hamilton. The rank was so meaningful to L'Enfant, and he clung so tightly to it for the rest of his life, that many of his contemporaries—especially those who knew him only from newspapers—could have believed that his first name was "Major" rather than Peter. That same month Continental Army officers formed The Society of the Cincinnati in order to maintain the bonds of friendship, promote their interests with government and aid the widows and orphans of deceased officers. L'Enfant became a founding member. Steuben, as the Society's temporary president, asked him to design its emblemology. The artist chose the bald eagle as a central motif because its range was limited to the North American continent, but surely the Roman imperial precedent influenced him as well. Henry Knox described the diploma to Washington as a "noble effort of genius."[10] A month later Louis XVI provided L'Enfant with a respectable military pension for life. Unfortunately the life that mattered turned out to be the King's and the pension disappeared like so much else during the French Revolution.

Later that summer Steuben selected L'Enfant to be the engineer on an abortive mission to Canada to inspect the Great Lakes forts and arrange for their transfer to the United States. L'Enfant, who had unsuccessfully tried to coax Superintendent of Finance Robert Morris "out of some money" in April 1782, was back for more in July 1783 prior to the Canadian trip. The engineer was quick to express his resentment when Morris again refused him any money in addition to his military pay. Eventually, after efforts by his friends Steuben and the Philadelphia merchant Thomas Fitzsimons, L'Enfant's Canadian expenses were covered.[11]

In October 1783 L'Enfant was at West Point where he received three hundred dollars from Society of the Cincinnati members for the purpose of having the medals and the copperplate for its diplomas struck in France. In granting permission for L'Enfant to be absent from the engineers to undertake the trip, Washington stressed that the designer was traveling on personal business and that the Society assumed none of the expenses of the trip other than the cost of producing the copperplate and medals, several of which Washington asked L'Enfant to purchase for him. Before leaving for his only visit back to France, which he reached in December 1783, L'Enfant made a courtesy call on the commander in chief when he was with Congress at Princeton, New Jersey, from 23 August until its adjournment on 3 November.[12]

Trans-Atlantic correspondence had been risky during the War, but L'Enfant and his family had done their best to keep in touch. At least once Charlotte Lenfant asked Benjamin Franklin, whom Congress had dispatched to join Silas Deane, to forward a letter to her son on the grounds that several had miscarried. Two of L'Enfant's letters, one to his parents and another to a friend, fell into the hands of the British and were turned over to the Loyalist newspaper editor and master forger James Rivington, who published both after crafting them into attacks on the absurd Americans, the faithless Congress and the cowardly Continental Army. Correspondence between L'Enfant and his parents and friends at home continued throughout the 1780s although not without problems. A February 1787 letter to his parents that suggested he might visit them in September went unanswered, neither did he hear from his servant who had returned to France in May, nor from any of the many friends he had written. The letter he sent his parents in September to say that he would not be coming reveals that he did not know that his father had died the previous month, an event that brought condolences from George Washington and a wish that "prosperity & felicity" be "attendant on all your steps." The loss of his father meant that the supply of money that had supported him since his arrival in America was also gone, a fact that intensified his habit of poor mouthing.

In the spring of 1788 L'Enfant wrote his mother, expressing concern about the retired life that she had been living at the Gobelins since becoming a widow. He also complained about his financial situation, reflecting "that nothing is more necessary for my own affairs than for me to come to France, and that by remaining in America not only do I lose advancement and employment … but I have nothing left to live on here, after all my sacrifices, than such small payments as may be made to me." The family had little if any contact during the turbulent 1790s when the French Revolution destroyed the way of life to which L'Enfant had been bred. After the turn of the century he heard from them again. In 1805 a cousin urged him to write his mother even if he could not send money, and, as a spur, informed him that his father had left him an inheritance. A year later another cousin wrote to inform the fifty-two year old L'Enfant that his mother had died.[13]

In France during the winter of 1783–84 L'Enfant visited the Marquis de Lafayette and at least one American, who informed Robert Morris that L'Enfant was like most Frenchmen returning home from abroad: "after a first visit they are no more heard of." L'Enfant carried out his assignment for the Society and secured special approval from Louis XVI for French officers to join the Society and wear its insignia. He arrived back in the United States in April 1784, fleeing his French creditors and leaving an embarrassing situation on the doorstep of the new American Ambassador, Thomas Jefferson. The engineer did not mention his money problems to Washington when detailing the success of his mission. Instead he turned to Alexander Hamilton, the man who more than any other became his patron, explaining that the necessity of appearing at Court in a manner consistent with the dignity of The Society of the Cincinnati had resulted in living expenses far beyond the amount projected. With Hamilton's support the Society agreed to cover the expenses. But it was not enough, and in 1786 L'Enfant submitted a forty page petition informing the Society that he was being prosecuted in Europe and that "my honor is hazarded." Two years later he appealed directly to Washington, reporting that failure to pay his French creditors had earned him the animosity of Lafayette who had consequently blocked a promised favor from the French Court.[14]

L'Enfant was officially discharged along with most of the Continental Army on 1 January 1784. Soon thereafter the federal government estimated that it owed him $29,323 in back pay, an amount that bore an annual interest of $1,759. He sought support from General Henry Knox for additional back pay covering the months that he had been in France, and for appointment as brigadier general to head an engineering department in the small post-war army maintained by Congress. The ambitious L'Enfant had something far greater in mind than the position previously held by Thaddeus Kosciuszko, which the Polish volunteer led L'Enfant to assume could be his for the asking.

Wishing to contribute to "the prosperity of a new Rising Empire" and render himself "useful in securing to the United States a peaceful and tranquil enjoyment of liberty," L'Enfant sent Congress a lengthy memorial with supporting documents in December 1784, urging it to establish a corps of engineers within a permanent military establishment. As a caution against the false security of peace so prevalent in neutral countries, he assigned the proposed department two primary duties: the fortification of harbors for both defense and the protection of trade, and the erection of frontier posts for the supervision of the Indian trade and the protection of Americans emigrating to the West. In addition he believed such a corps should have responsibility for all fortified places, all civil and military federal buildings, and all roads and bridges within the United States. As a capstone it should be charged with the long term project of producing an atlas of the entire continent for the use of the federal government. At the last minute, as we shall see, L'Enfant appended construction of the seat of federal government to the corps's proposed assignments.

An aggressive self-promoter and never one to neglect stressing his personal sacrifice—particularly financial—on behalf of the United States, L'Enfant indicated in his memorial that by remaining in America in hopes of such a department being established, he had lost the opportunity of employment in France. His memorial's inclusion of a separate discussion of the expertise required for an engineer provides a vivid and comprehensive description of the profession as L'Enfant understood it:

arithmetic, geometry, "mechanism" (i.e., physics), architecture, hydraulics, drawing, and natural philosophy, by which he meant an understanding of environmental quality as well as chemistry, materials science, and structural engineering. L'Enfant's concern about air and water pollution indicates that he was far ahead of his time as an engineer. Although he had acquired a "little theoretical knowledge … by study," L'Enfant had not been trained in the field. He was however surely familiar with the French engineering "system," from which town planning and architecture were just emerging as separate disciplines.

The memorial stands as a magnificent early American state paper, expressing the vision of a man who believed that American prospects and prosperity would depend entirely on the first measures the United States took to establish its character and credit. Although L'Enfant was careful to state that he was "well impregnated with the spirit of Republican Government," the proposal clearly exhibited the hallmarks of the information-gathering, statist tradition of government that had evolved in France since Charlemagne. Congress gave the memorial the dignity due a war hero by submitting it to a committee. Unfortunately L'Enfant's timing was politically disastrous, for Congress had been taken over by men who believed that the federal government should exercise only minimal responsibilities. A federal internal improvements program was far from their minds, except as a threat to the rights of the states they represented. The proposed corps's federal structure—it was to be divided into state units—and the memorial's careful homage to the concept of federalism, with examples of how the department would benefit the states as well as the "Continental Supreme power," did not convince the committee. It reported that the United States did not need a department of engineers. The advocate was not to be so easily discouraged and two months later, in congratulating Knox on his appointment as secretary at war, L'Enfant again called on him to support the creation of such a department under L'Enfant's command.[15]

At the same time that L'Enfant submitted his memorial, Congress chose New York City as the seat of federal government. This apparently spurred the engineer to move there as well and New York remained his home for the rest of the 1780s (and for several winters during the 1790s). Welcomed by such prominent residents as Alexander Hamilton, it was probably the happiest period of L'Enfant's life in the United States. He was befriended by the French Ambassador, the Comte de Moustier, who kindly made several requests on his behalf with the French government. "If I were easy enough in my mind to enjoy the pleasures of society," he informed his mother, Moustier's "charming sister-in-law, the Marquise de Bréhan, would make any man happy."[16]

At New York L'Enfant supported himself as an artist and architect. In October and November 1785 he assisted Jean-Antoine Houdon, who

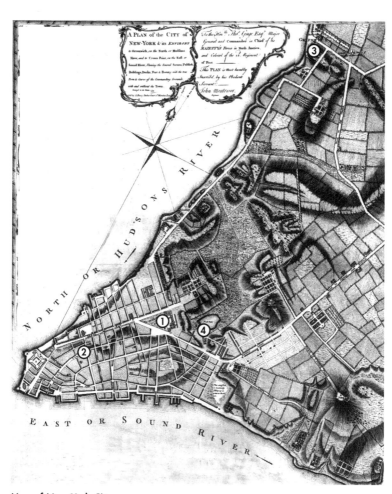

Map of New York City
The famous "Montresor map" of Lower Manhattan Island shows New York City much as L'Enfant would have found it when he settled there in 1784. Although the survey upon which the map is based was conducted in 1766, eight years' occupation of the besieged city by British troops had prevented its growth much farther north and east of the "Common" ① (site of the present day City Hall). The old City Hall ②, which L'Enfant remodeled into the city's architectural masterpiece, is at the head of Broad Street, near the geographic center of the city. The remainder of Manhattan Island below Greenwich (Village) ③ was part of a proposed grand real estate development for which L'Enfant designed a large park that extended northeast from the Fresh Water Pond ④.
(Courtesy of The New–York Historical Society, New York City)

was in the United States to take a life mask of George Washington and to obtain the commission to design an equestrian statue of Washington. Congress had authorized such a monument in August 1783, but it would not be executed until the nineteenth century when it was placed on the northwest corner of The George Washington University campus. L'Enfant designed the reredos at Saint Paul's Chapel and supervised the erection of the statue of General Richard Montgomery in front of the church. Later he made ornamental additions to the statue's pediment, which a newspaper writer, capitalizing on a ready pun, described as so tawdry, absurd, bizarre, and disgraceful to taste as to "even discredit the mind d'un enfant." The vestry rose to L'Enfant's defense with a resolution describing the work as reflecting "honor on his taste."[17] Documentation for most of his other New York projects is minimal.

At the end of the decade a company of land speculators inspired by the real estate speculator William Duer asked L'Enfant to lay out a huge development that spanned Manhattan Island between New York City and Greenwich Village. As its centerpiece L'Enfant designed a large pictur-esque park surrounding the fresh water pond just northeast of Chambers Street and extending north to encompass Bunker Hill at Grand Street. In addition to several rows of large houses in and around the park, the hilly area was to be landscaped with forest trees.[18] L'Enfant's design has not been found, but the description of it indicates that it was an important precursor of Central Park. Even less well documented is his work as an architect and builder of private homes. He is alleged to have designed and overseen the construction of several in northern New Jersey and New York City, allegedly employing the young Duncan Phyfe to do the interior cabinetwork after Phyfe moved to New York City in 1790. L'Enfant later claimed that by 1790 he was "affluent … and able of commanding what-ever business I liked," enough so that he had abandoned tavern living and maintained a house, servants and horses, a very different situation than the one he had described to his mother two years earlier.[19]

Two of the architect's building proposals remain mysteries. In January 1787 William Temple Franklin wrote L'Enfant that Philadelphians were "determined upon erecting [a] building similar" to the one L'Enfant had proposed for a "society" in New York City, the plan for which Franklin had earlier seen. L'Enfant replied exuberantly, asking for details about the location and size of the lot on which the building would stand, estimating the cost at just below $20,000, and proposing to surround the outside of the building "with small shops under cover of a gallery" similar to those Franklin had seen "in the piazzas that surround the comedie francaise … or that sur-round the palais Roial" when he was with his famous grandfather in Paris. Not only would the effect be "grand," but the shops would be practical because their rent would soon make up the cost of the entire building or at least bring a good interest for the money borrowed to build it. One hypo-thesis as to what building was meant is that Franklin was acting on behalf of Philadelphians planning to build a new city and county courthouse. The commissioners of the city and county of Philadelphia presented plans to the state government in March 1787 and won its approval for constructing the

New York City's Grand Parade

New York's "Grand Federal Procession" of 23 July 1788 was actually the city's annual July 4th celebration thrice postponed in hopes that the state convention would ratify the new federal Constitution. L'Enfant choreographed the elaborate public ritual, accounts of which circulated in newspapers from New Hampshire to Virginia. Approximately 5,000 marchers (almost one quarter of the city's residents) participated in the mile and a half long parade. The order consisted of eight delegations of tradesmen with occupational emblems and representative floats, followed by lawyers, merchants, and Columbia College students and faculty, and trailed lastly by physicians, foreign dignitaries, and militia. Near the middle of the procession ten horses pulled a 27 foot long miniature frigate christened the *Hamilton*, manned by sailors and marines firing 32 guns. If this 19th century engraving is an accurate depiction of the float's complexity, it almost certainly defied L'Enfant's own knowledge of naval engineering to design. (Stephen L. Schechter, ed., *The Reluctant Pillar: New York and the Adoption of the Federal Constitution* [Troy, N.Y., 1985], pp. 112-13) (Courtesy of The New-York Historical Society, New York City)

building on the northwest corner of State House Square, just to the west of the Pennsylvania State House (Independence Hall). The architect is unknown. Construction began in July and was completed in March 1789; Congress met in the building from December 1790 until it adjourned to Washington, D.C. in May 1800. If this hypothesis is correct, it implies that the New York "society" that approached L'Enfant in the late 1780s sought to build a new city hall.[20]

"an allegory to the new constitution"

In September 1787 the Federal Convention proposed a new and revolutionary constitution for the United States that made the federal government supreme over the states. The document had the active support of L'Enfant's friend Alexander Hamilton and most of the other Continental Army officers with whom the architect associated. On 23 July 1788 L'Enfant directed the grand parade in New York City celebrating its ratification by the states; he also designed the parade's iconography and some of its floats, perhaps including the federal ship "Hamilton," as well as the banquet pavilion on Bunker Hill where hundreds dined before the evening's fireworks. "The taste and genius of Major L'Enfant, so often displayed on public occasions, were never more conspicuous," recalled one of the observers sixty years later.[21] Probably a labor of love, his well received efforts that day set him up for a very special commission. The Confederation Congress decided in mid-September 1788 that the new government under the Constitution should convene at New York. In response, the New York City Common Council chose L'Enfant to remodel City Hall at Wall, Nassau, and Broad Streets for the accommodation of Congress.

Federal Hall, as his elegant building became known, was a triumph. But it was to be the last known professional project that he would see through to completion. He was able to complete it partly because the Council had the wisdom to appoint the architect one of five commissioners charged with superintending construction. A second reason for his success was the fact that, for once, money was not an issue. The stakes were too high. While both natives and visitors alike marveled at New York's civic-minded willingness to expend over $50,000 on a public building, most recognized that it was the City's best weapon to insure that the First Federal Congress would not succumb to the incessant pressure from the Pennsylvanians and their allies to move the seat of federal government to Philadelphia. Indeed, some congressmen referred to Federal Hall as "Fool's Trap." Pennsylvania Senator William Maclay considered it insulting that anyone thought the federal government should stay at New York merely because of "the Jimcrackery and Gingerbread of an old building new vamped up." He nicknamed Federal Hall the "Great

L'Enfant's Pavilion

Where the "Grand Federal Procession" terminated at the city's parade grounds on the slopes of "Bunker Hill" (near the present day intersection of Grand Street and The Bowery), 6,000 celebrants were treated to a banquet hosted by the various trade associations at a pavilion designed by L'Enfant. As shown here in a contemporary drawing by David Grim (1737-1826), the pavilion consisted of ten 440 foot long tables radiating outward to form a half circle whose "hub" was three smaller pavilions connected by a 150 foot colonnade; members of the Confederation Congress were seated in the middle, foreign diplomats on the right and clergymen and government officials on the left. (Stephen L. Schechter, ed., *The Reluctant Pillar: New York and the Adoption of the Federal Constitution* [Troy, N.Y., 1985], pp. 113) (Courtesy of The New-York Historical Society, New York City)

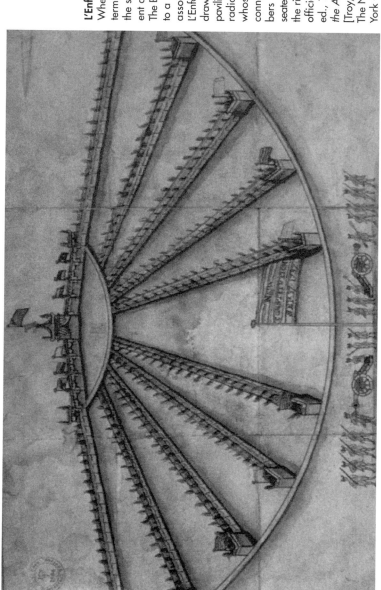

Baby House," and promised in an anonymous newspaper parody not to employ "infants" to build a fitting house for Congress if it left New York.[22]

As construction began at the end of September, Steuben informed his close friend William North that "poor" L'Enfant "gives himself a great deal of pain" about the project—all "pour la Gloire," for the sake of glory. Two hundred artisans, carpenters and unskilled laborers worked on the site. Presumably many of the laborers were immigrants, like the French Ambassador's servant who obtained the contract for the interior upholstery. The idea of such a windfall benefitting foreign workers instead of native citizens was a source of resentment for at least one editorial writer who faulted L'Enfant's "prepossession in favor of foreigners (even of the lowest class)." Whether by prepossession or disposition, the architect throughout his career demonstrated an unusual ability to work with the laborers responsible for turning his plans into realities, ensuring in this instance the completion of the renovated Senate Chamber and the near completion of the exterior by the end of the first week of January 1789.

By February the major construction had been completed on L'Enfant's *piece de resistance*: the new House Chamber with its extraordinary forty-six foot high coved ceiling, its large windows sixteen feet above the floor and its two spectators' galleries. The unfinished facade was festooned with flags to commemorate the birth of the new government on 4 March, and the crowning glory, the eagle on the pediment, was installed by 22 April. L'Enfant arranged for cabinetmakers to provide furniture for the clerk of the House and the secretary of the Senate. One cannot help but speculate that it was L'Enfant who decided to devote the second floor lobby of Federal Hall to an art gallery and to include works by his friend John Trumbull.[23]

On 30 April George Washington was inaugurated as the first president of the United States at Federal Hall on the balcony overlooking Wall Street, festooned with a red and white fabric especially designed for the occasion by L'Enfant. Congress appointed the architect as one of seven special "Assistants" to make arrangements and provide security for the ceremony, but for some reason L'Enfant declined the honor. Given his dreams for the United States and his hopes for federal employment, this was perhaps the most bizarre decision of his life. It surely resulted from some perceived insult to his sense of honor—not having a more important role in planning the event for example—or from some violation of his vision of how Federal Hall should be used for inaugurations. It is even possible that wounded pride kept him from attending the event itself. A more notable absence was Martha Washington, whose precedent modern first ladies have not found expedient to follow. Soon after she arrived at New York a month later, L'Enfant gave her a private tour of his masterpiece.[24]

Broad Street Cityscape
This watercolor on paper, drawn by George Holland around 1797, is the view of the north end of Broad Street most contemporaneous with L'Enfant's work on Federal Hall, which crowns the scene in the distance. It shows the architect's grand style in stark contrast to the cramped and gothic look of the surrounding buildings, some of which dated to the seventeenth century. Part of the effect is due to the artist's deliberate distortion of the bend in Broad Street, which actually occurs further to the south, leaving a straighter, more direct and sweeping approach to Federal Hall where it intersected with Wall Street. Rising to the left is the steeple of St. Paul's at Broadway and Partition Street, which was not completed until 1794 and would not have appeared in the vista while Congress was meeting at Federal Hall. (Courtesy of the I.N. Phelps Stokes Collection, New York Public Library)

L'Enfant and Federal Hall could not be praised enough, particularly by New Yorkers. "There is no public building in the Union equal to it" observed the postmaster general. New York's mayor wrote L'Enfant "that while the Hall exists it will exhibit a most respectable monument of your eminent talents." The *New–York Packet* applauded the architect and master workmen for their "extraordinary exertions" in nearly completing the "superb building" within only five months, "notwithstanding the inclemency of the season"; its grandeur struck all "with pleasure and surprise, as it far exceeds their most sanguine expectations." A poem in another newspaper suggested that the Antifederalists who opposed the Constitution must be piqued—apparently no New Yorker could be truly "angered" at L'Enfant—about the magic art that converted a "gothic heap" into such a "lovely building." A year after Congress occupied it, an official advertisement declared that Federal Hall did "honor to the architect."[25]

The French Ambassador was especially taken with L'Enfant's achievement and informed Versailles that, "under the pretext of a few necessary changes," he had modified the old building bit by bit so that it "retained only its name. In the end he created a monument that can serve as an allegory to the new constitution. Both have been entirely changed by their architects, who brought their clients a great deal further than they had thought to go." The architect had not been "guided or bothered by anyone. Amendments were proposed to him (as to the new Constitution). He listened to all the advice, and followed his own ideas."[26] Architectural historian Pamela Scott credits L'Enfant's Federal Hall as "a harbinger of more flexible and cosmopolitan public buildings for America." In addition, she points out that his novel use of familiar American symbols throughout the building, including the "invention of an American order—columns with their accompanying capitals and entablature," initiated "a national emblematic language" in both architectural forms and decorative details.[27]

Federal Hall immediately joined the eagle and thirteen of almost anything as a prominent element of American patriotic iconography. At the John Street Theater in July 1789, an image of Federal Hall emerged from the clouds to the accompaniment of swelling music, while an actor dressed as the "genius of Columbia" addressed it as "that Temple, sacred to patriotism, liberty and virtue." By 1790 attending the House debates at Federal Hall had become the most popular social activity in New York for tourists and natives with leisure. Poet Philip Freneau published "Federal Hall" in March in recognition of the phenomenon. The building also assumed a prominent place in at least two political cartoons hawked on New York's streets during the successful campaign to move the seat of federal government to Philadelphia. Just after Congress left the city in August a New Yorker suggested that the key to the Bastille, which the Marquis de Lafayette had sent to George Washington, ought to

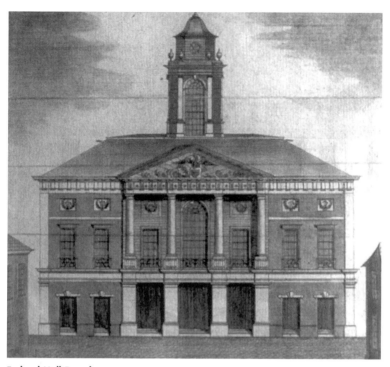

Federal Hall Facade

The Massachusetts Magazine of June 1789 published the fullest contemporary description of Federal Hall; its accompanying engraving by Samuel Hill is acknowledged to be the most accurate illustration. This may in part be due to the skilled eye of Charles Bulfinch (1763–1844), who was in New York City at the time of Washington's first inaugural and is credited with making the drawing upon which Hill's engraving is based. There is perhaps some poetic justice in the likelihood that our best idea of what the first U.S. capitol looked like in 1789 is due to the architect responsible for completing the permanent Capitol thirty-seven years later. (Louis Torres, "Federal Hall Revisited," *Journal of the Society of Architectural Historians* 29(1970):332) (Courtesy of The New–York Historical Society, New York City)

be displayed there. But local pride in the building and its history quickly waned and when Federal Hall was torn down in 1812 the salvaged materials sold at auction for $425.[28]

In March 1790 the State of New York, in a last ditch effort to convince Congress to remain in New York City, appropriated $20,000 for the construction of a grand residence at the foot of Manhattan Island for the president of the United States. When it advertised for an architect, it was natural to assume that L'Enfant would use the opportunity to again "display his genius" and "taste." "I have no doubt he will erect an edifice which will do honor to the city of New–York," commented a newspaper writer. But this was not to be the case, for L'Enfant had become embittered. In October 1789 the New York Common Council had adopted a resolution expressing its appreciation to him and declaring him an honorary freeman of the city. In March 1790 it presented him with ten acres of land (between what would become 66th and 70th Streets just east of Third Avenue) as compensation for his work. When asked by the Council if it were true as rumored that he did not want the land, the architect responded curtly that the rumor was "perfectly agreeable with my sentiments and disposition to refuse the gift."[29]

L'Enfant surely considered the vacant land paltry compensation and an insult to his honor. Coming from a European tradition in which great success was richly rewarded by the Court, L'Enfant had accepted the Federal Hall project under the naive assumption that the same would be true in America. It was a lesson the architect should not have had to learn personally. He was well aware of the problems his fellow European by birth, Frederick Steuben, was experiencing in his efforts to extract from Congress what he considered just compensation for his wartime services. And it was a lesson L'Enfant did not learn—ever. Nowhere is this better seen than in the context of the events that underlay his resurrection in the late nineteenth century—and reburial in the early twentieth—as "Pierre" Charles L'Enfant, the Frenchman who designed Washington, D.C. The details of the planner's experience with the federal city from March 1791 through February 1792 have been described elsewhere in far greater detail than is appropriate here, but some modifications of those accounts are in order.

"TO GIVE AN IDEA OF THE GREATNESS OF THE EMPIRE"

The founders of the sectionally-divided United States fought long and hard over the location of the permanent seat of federal government. Congressional debate began in 1783 and was resolved that year with a decision to build two federal towns: one to the North near Trenton, New Jersey, and another to the South near Georgetown, Maryland. That decision was rescinded a year later in favor of a single federal town near Trenton. The town was never built because southern congressmen, encouraged by George Washington, easily blocked appropriations for the project. A contentious debate over whether to locate it on the Potomac or Susquehanna River consumed the House of Representatives in September 1789 before it narrowly decided on the latter site. When the Senate named the suburbs of Philadelphia instead, Rep. James Madison of Virginia successfully engineered a postponement of the bill until the next session, at which time Congress adopted a rule declaring that all business died when a session ended.

The issue was finally resolved in July 1790 when President Washington signed the Residence Act locating the seat of government on the Potomac River. Southerners achieved this victory after seven years of struggle because of the Compromise of 1790. By the terms of that Compromise, the New England States agreed to drop their opposition to the Potomac River location; in exchange, the South agreed to provide the few votes needed to include a provision for federal assumption of most of the Revolutionary War debt of the states in the Funding Act implementing Secretary of the Treasury Alexander Hamilton's report on public credit. The Compromise ultimately proved a high price for the agricultural and states rights-minded South because it established the constitutional doctrine of implied powers and the form of economic organization known as financial capitalism.[30]

As the final congressional debate over the location of the seat of federal government occurred in the about-to-be abandoned Federal Hall, a satirical newspaper piece reported that a member of Congress, advocating a seat that moved from state to state, proposed that L'Enfant design a state house on wheels. The Residence Act provided that Congress sit in Philadelphia until 1800, stimulating one of its congressmen, L'Enfant's friend Thomas Fitzsimons, to recommend that the designer of Federal Hall, who very much wanted the proposed commission, be hired either to renovate one of Philadelphia's public buildings or erect a new one for Congress. The recommendation touted the architect as a mild mannered and unassuming man who would not expect too high a compensation and who worked well with common laborers. Along with the French Ambassador's assessment that L'Enfant had proven with Federal Hall "not only his talent as an artist, but moreover his intelligence with regard to the people he was dealing with," the recommendation can be read as a valediction to a triumphant career. Things would never be the same again.[31]

Since at least 1784, the always ambitious L'Enfant had had his eye on the commission as designer and superintendent of construction for the federal town—or federal city as it came to be known among those who supported a powerful federal government. (Washington, D.C., would not be called the "Capital" for almost a century except by its promoters in the 1790s, its later residents, and facetiously by others.) Congress had been in the midst of one of its debates on the location of the seat of government in December 1784 when L'Enfant submitted his memorial proposing that Congress create a corps of army engineers. He quickly appended an argument for making construction of the federal seat one of its special responsibilities. With the keen foresight that distinguished his ideas, the engineer insisted that creating a proper seat of government for the United States would take years and a great amount of money because it must be accomplished in "such a manner as to give an idea of the greatness of the empire as well as to engrave in every mind that sense of respect due to a place which is the seat of a supreme sovereignty." Hiring workers and supplying them as needed for particular aspects of the noble project was wasteful of Congress's time and money. Assigning the responsibility to his proposed corps would not only

Cartoon

Several unsigned cartoons ferociously protested Congress's decision in July 1790 to abandon New York as the temporary seat of government. An early example shows Pennsylvania Senator Robert Morris, led by the devil, en route to Philadelphia with Federal Hall on his shoulders. A man in woman's clothing introduces himself to a Philadelphia prostitute as a procuress for Congress, while a congressional chaplain promises to pray wherever he was paid. Satirical representations of other congressmen as well as specific judicial and executive officers were added in variant versions of this colorful and widely circulated cartoon. Ironically, Morris—the man New Yorkers most harshly vilified for rendering Federal Hall obsolete—later became one of its architect's most stalwart friends and patrons. (Courtesy of the American Antiquarian Society, Worcester, Mass.)

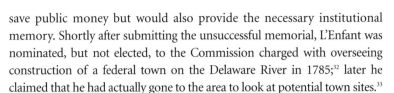

save public money but would also provide the necessary institutional memory. Shortly after submitting the unsuccessful memorial, L'Enfant was nominated, but not elected, to the Commission charged with overseeing construction of a federal town on the Delaware River in 1785;[32] later he claimed that he had actually gone to the area to look at potential town sites.[33]

During the intense debate over the location of the seat of government in the House of Representatives in September 1789, L'Enfant pulled out his 1784 memorial and modified it into a letter to President Washington, the spelling and syntax of which indicate that it was put into final form by someone else, most probably Hamilton. L'Enfant began by observing that the decision "to lay the foundation of a Federal City which is to become the Capital of this vast Empire, offers so great an occasion for acquiring reputation … that Your Excellency will not be surprised that my ambition and the desire I have of becoming a useful citizen should lead me to wish to share in the undertaking." "No nation had ever before the opportunity offered them of deliberately deciding on the spot where their Capital City should be fixed," he continued, and "although the means now within the power of the Country are not such as to pursue the design to any great extent, it will be obvious that the plan should be drawn on such a scale as to leave room for that aggrandizement and embellishment which the increase of the wealth of the Nation will permit it to pursue at any period however remote." L'Enfant, while asking that Washington employ him in the business, also took the opportunity to advocate for his dream job, a permanent army corps of engineers headed by himself as Engineer to the United States.[34]

After Congress finally made its decision on the location in 1790, Secretary of the Treasury Hamilton recommended L'Enfant to Washington as the best person available to plan the city. Much less enthusiastic was Thomas Jefferson who proved to be a key player in the decision-making process as secretary of state when that department had responsibility for many federal domestic functions now distributed elsewhere. As involved as he was with the project, he would have been even more so had Washington not been emotionally incapable of refraining from its micro management. L'Enfant's reputation must have given Jefferson pause, for the secretary had a strong bias in favor of "smaller is better." He was certainly not pleased when he saw L'Enfant's plan for a grand city that encompassed 6,000 acres and glowed with an iconography of federal supremacy. This was a sharp contrast to the town that Jefferson wished to see built on approximately fifty acres between present day Seventeenth Street, Twenty Third Street, D Street, and Constitution Avenue, just south of The George Washington University. While Jefferson surely recalled the debts L'Enfant had left at his door in France in 1784, his suspicions about the plan and the planner did not arise from the fact that L'Enfant was a member of The Society of the Cincinnati.

Contemporaries recognized that the construction of a federal city became Washington's "hobby horse," and his preeminent biographer concludes that even if he had had no other responsibilities as president he could not have devoted more time to the project. Nevertheless the law required that he appoint a presidential commission—a new and untried institution in federal government—to oversee the work and he did so on 22 January 1791. Washington chose three men who would do his bidding: Virginian David Stuart, a former state legislator, was the administrator of Washington's private business affairs, the husband of Martha Washington's widowed daughter-in-law, and the only person to whom the president wrote candid political letters; former governor of Maryland Thomas Johnson, the congressman who had nominated Washington to be commander in chief of the Continental Army; and Daniel Carroll of Rock Creek who had just been defeated by Marylanders furious over his support for seating the federal government at a location where it was thought it would benefit Virginia more than Maryland. Like Washington, all three were members of the Potomac Navigation Company. Johnson and Stuart in particular had devoted considerable time to implementing its plans to render the Potomac River the preeminent water route from the Atlantic Ocean to the West. Within a week of their appointment and weeks before they met, Jefferson informed the commissioners that Washington had selected L'Enfant to make a map of the ground so that locations for the public buildings could be determined.[35]

L'Enfant, who arrived at Georgetown on 9 March, was described by the local newspaper as "Major Longfont a French gentleman employed by the President of the United States to survey the lands" where the federal city is to be built. "His skill in matters of this kind is justly extolled by all disposed to give merits its proper tribute of praise." At Georgetown the planner met and came under the influence of the merchant George Walker, the exuberant local promoter who two years earlier had proposed in a newspaper article the exact location and size of the city, the means of acquiring the land and financing construction, and several of the institutions included in L'Enfant's plan. But the design was entirely L'Enfant's conception and, because of the burst of creative energy that marked the beginning of all his projects, he had a draft on paper to show to Washington when the president arrived only two weeks later. Because L'Enfant's papers relating to the plan were rifled, scattered and apparently lost, we shall never have a fully detailed explication of what he had in mind. Clearly his capital of magnificent buildings and commercial facilities reflected an optimistic outlook for the survival of the Union and the establishment of a republican commercial empire.

It was a vision shared enthusiastically by Washington, the man who dispatched L'Enfant to the Potomac and to whom L'Enfant considered himself responsible. In fact, L'Enfant later claimed that before his

Garnet W. Jex, *The Planning of Washington, 1791* (1931) [Detail], Oil on canvas, 60″ x 84″.
In his George Washington University M.F.A. thesis, Garnet W. Jex combined elements of the ascendant American impressionism school with the genre style of historical painting popular a half century earlier. It is a bold and novel composition. In order to pay tribute to so many historical actors in a single work of art, Jex invoked artistic license to portray them at a fictitious meeting in the spring of 1791 near the present intersection of Pennsylvania Ave. and L. St., N.W. From left to right: Federal City Commissioners David Stuart, Thomas Johnson, and Daniel Carroll; the Capitol's future architect, Dr. William Thornton; L'Enfant; Washington; and the surveyors Andrew Ellicott and Benjamin Banneker. Jex's conscientious research and inference yielded reliable likenesses in all but one instance: the robust African-American who seems to be holding someone's horse was in reality a 60 year old rheumatic astronomer who maintained the survey team's sophisticated equipment and made the celestial calculations on which the boundaries of the District of Columbia are based. (© The George Washington University, 2002, The George Washington University Permanent Collection, Courtesy of the Luther Brady Art Gallery)

appointment was announced he made frequent trips to Philadelphia at his own expense during the winter of 1790–91 to consult with Washington about the project.[36] This suggests that Washington had more influence on the plan than previously realized and adds force to L'Enfant's oft repeated phrase that he had undertaken at the federal city the execution of the president's intentions. Alexander Hamilton's commercial vision for the United States can clearly be seen in the plan, but it remains unclear to what extent L'Enfant's ideas about a commercial republic were arrived at independently of his friend. Several impressive articles about the plan and L'Enfant's intentions have been written by architectural historians.[37]

George Washington suffered from "Potomac Fever," in those days a delusion-inducing obsession with the beauty and commercial potential of the Potomac River. The Fever was hereditary, and the Washington, Lee, Carroll, and Digges families of the Potomac upper tidewater were the most prominent to be infected. In addition, Washington believed passionately that the location he had personally selected for the seat of federal government was the best site anywhere in the United States for empowering the federal government, guaranteeing the survival of the Union, and ensuring his reputation in its history. Enraptured, and surely loquacious when sharing the draft plan with Washington, L'Enfant persuaded the president to accept Walker's grand 6,000 acre proposal. It was undoubtedly an easy sell, and the president quickly became wedded to L'Enfant's vision of the city and remained so throughout his life. But Washington was a realist and L'Enfant, despite the long-range view in his 1784 memorial to Congress and his 1789 letter to Washington, was not. Consequently the president recognized that it would take a century to raise the kind of city he and his planner envisioned.[38] Finally, Walker's scheme freed the president from having to make a difficult political choice between two rival groups of landowners— or proprietors as they came to be known—over whether to site the public buildings near Georgetown or closer to the Eastern Branch of the Potomac (Anacostia River). L'Enfant's proposal to separate by more than a mile the presidential mansion and the Capitol, the two major public buildings for which he expected to be the architect, would please both groups and make the plan easier to sell when Washington sought to acquire the land in question for the public.

When John Trumbull and Rep. William Loughton Smith passed through the area in the spring of 1791, the enthusiastic L'Enfant gave the men tours of the site. To Smith he proclaimed that "nature has done much for it, and with the aid of art it will become the wonder of the world." The planner must have been convincing, for the well-traveled Smith, who found the grand, romantic vistas enchanting, concluded that this "new Seat of Empire, Washingtonople" held more advantages for its

L'Enfant's Plan

This is a detail from a computer assisted reproduction (1991) of the heavily annotated manuscript map that L'Enfant first laid before President Washington around 26 August 1791. Originally, a cartouche that appeared in the upper left corner may not have included his name. The words "By Peter Charles L'Enfant" (significantly, utilizing the anglicized version of the designer's name) appear squeezed in at a slight angle and in a different hand than the rest of the lettering, suggesting it was probably added sometime between 26 August and 13 December, when Washington finally presented the map to Congress. (Courtesy of the Library of Congress, Washington, D.C.)

proposed purpose than any place he had seen in the United States. In April L'Enfant wrote Jefferson indicating that Washington had approved the plan and "left to me without any restriction whatsoever" to delineate it. To his friend Hamilton he was much more effusive. He had been too busy to write because of "the most fatiguing work which I ever had to perform—that of surveying at so improper [a] season of the year." While apprehensive that he would be considered too partial to the site, he insisted in words, which could just as easily have been those of Washington, "that no position in all America can be more susceptible of grand improvement, more capable of promoting the rapid increases of a city nor better situated to secure an infinity of advantage to government." So consumed by the design of the city was L'Enfant that the secretary of the treasury had to remind him not to forget a request to direct his imagination to the design of America's first coins.[39]

L'Enfant recognized the importance of politics in American society even if he was incapable of modifying his own behavior accordingly. Assisting Washington's private secretary Tobias Lear in purchasing a lot in the federal city, the planner urged him to interest his fellow New Englanders in investing in the project and moving to the city rather than to the West. "If the opposers to the measure" would set aside their local bias, "they would agree with me that it is a most eligible one for to fix upon the capital of this extensive empire," despite the fact that in its origin "it was not a matter of choice but a result of party spirit and in a great measure of a collusion of local view … one of the most glaring instances amongst the few when petit motives has prompted a grand interest." Like Washington, the designer believed the city would provide a venue for northerners and southerners to mingle familiarly and thus contribute to the survival of the Union.[40]

L'Enfant worked closely with Washington throughout the summer of 1791 as they refined the city plan, both men seemingly oblivious to the existence of the Commission that on 8 September named the federal city (the area delineated by present day Florida Avenue, Rock Creek, and the Anacostia River) "The City of Washington" and the entire one hundred square mile district "The District of Columbia." In December Washington submitted the plan, credited to "Peter Charles L'Enfant" in the cartouche, to Congress. One newspaper writer condemned it as overly grand, while another observed several years later that "poor Mr. L'Enfant" would perhaps eventually be "censured for sacrificing so much ground to public purposes" instead of private housing. George Walker could not praise the plan enough in an anonymous September 1791 newspaper article, the first public description. Walker called the site the most beautiful, salubrious and convenient in America if not in the world, predicting that the federal city would rise with a rapidity previously unparalleled in urban history, that it would become the delight and admiration of the world, and that future generations would consider it

Andrew Ellicott's Map
The fieldwork for the first map of the entire ten miles square federal district was completed in December 1792, under the direction of Andrew Ellicott with the assistance of several men, including L'Enfant, who helped survey the water courses in the vicinity of the city itself. After re-surveying some roads and waterways, Ellicott completed a six-sheet manuscript map on 25 June 1793, which was the basis for the single-sheet engraving shown here, submitted to the president on 28 February 1794—two years after L'Enfant's resignation. The district's dramatic topography, vividly depicted by Ellicott, heavily influenced L'Enfant's overall design. The city itself is splayed out upon the basin between the Potomac and the Eastern Branch, here labeled for the first time the "Annakostia" at Secretary of State Jefferson's urging, in acknowledgment of the original Native American presence. (Courtesy of the Library of Congress, Washington, D.C.)

one of George Washington's greatest accomplishments. The L'Enfant plan "exhibits such striking proofs of an exalted genius, elegance of taste, extensive imagination and comprehension, as will not only produce amazement in Europe, but meet the admiration of all future ages." Walker continued to promote the plan in the United States and abroad until he, like several of the early proprietors of the federal city, went broke.[41]

At the construction site the situation was less positive. L'Enfant must not have been pleased with at least three of the decisions reached at a late August 1791 meeting that the president held with Jefferson and

Madison: a prize competition would be held for architects interested in submitting proposals for the public buildings, no public squares other than for those for the Capitol and the executive buildings would be developed at first, and internal improvements such as the canal and a bridge over the Eastern Branch of the Potomac (Anacostia River) would be postponed until money became available.[42] More serious were the disagreements that arose between L'Enfant and the Commission as it began to assert its prerogatives in the fall of 1791.

L'Enfant purchased a lot at the first sale in October, but refused to make his map available to the Commission and potential buyers on the grounds that if he did so only the best lots would be purchased and these probably by speculators rather than individuals more committed to the City of Washington. Jefferson unsuccessfully urged Washington to use the opportunity to instruct L'Enfant that he was subordinate to the Commission. Then, in November, L'Enfant tore down part of a house under construction that projected seven feet into his planned New Jersey Avenue, SE. It was the property of the politically influential Daniel Carroll of Duddington, a distant cousin of Commissioner Daniel Carroll of Rock Creek. The president quickly became embroiled with Carroll, whom he thought in the wrong, L'Enfant, whom he thought lacked political sense, and the Commission. Both incidents were symptoms of a larger problem. Always sensitive to slight, L'Enfant bristled at what he considered the Commission's lack of support for his grand plan and its refusal to rely on him for matters within his professional competence. And he had little respect for the three politicians who composed it. To L'Enfant's mind they were too dull to understand his plan. Loquacious as he was, L'Enfant made his opinions known to the bachelor proprietors at Georgetown with whom he associated, calling the commissioners ignorant and unfit. Ferociously defensive of his plan, he even made the absurd accusation that they did not have the cause of the federal city at heart. For their part, the commissioners, who heard what L'Enfant had said about them, considered him demeaning and insolent and his plan grandiose and expensive.[43]

For Washington a potential political disaster loomed because a dispute between L'Enfant and the Commission threatened the *absolute* necessity that the city be ready for the federal government in 1800 so that its enemies could not argue in favor of remaining at Philadelphia. Jefferson drafted the president's 2 December letter of reprimand to L'Enfant: "I wished you to be employed in the arrangements of the Federal City: I still wish it: but only on condition that you conduct yourself in subordination to the authority of the Commissioners." At this point Washington added "to whom by law the business is entrusted, and who stands between you and the President of the United States." This was impossible for L'Enfant to accept since Washington had personally assigned him the job and had worked closely with him on the plan for at least six months without the slightest involvement of the commissioners. Ten days later Washington again stressed to the city planner the legal necessity of his subordination to the Commission.[44]

At the same time, Washington encouraged the commissioners to be considerate of L'Enfant and his great genius. Prior to his December letters to the planner, he had written David Stuart, the commissioner with whom he communicated privately, "that it is much to be regretted—however common the case is—that men who possess talents which fit them for peculiar purposes should almost invariably be under the influence of untoward dispositions." Nonetheless, Washington continued, from "my first knowledge" of L'Enfant's "abilities in the line of his profession, I have viewed him not only as a scientific man, but one who added considerable taste to his professional knowledge; and that, for such employment as he is now engaged in, for projecting public works, and carrying them into effect, he was better qualified than any one, who had come within my knowledge in this Country."[45]

L'Enfant went to Philadelphia at the end of 1791 to have the plan engraved and to talk with the foreign ambassadors and consuls about the willingness of their governments to pay for constructing embassies. In mid January he made a lengthy detailed report to the president (pointedly not to the Commission) that included plans for future work, an estimate of costs, proposals for financing, a redefinition of the chain of command, and thoughts on the political importance of proceeding expeditiously. Washington officially ignored the report, but he was so committed to L'Enfant's vision that he allowed the situation to remain unresolved for a month as he tried by every means at his disposal to retain L'Enfant. Learning that George Walker was in Philadelphia, the president sought him out as a mediator, but the effort led nowhere. On 22 February Jefferson informed L'Enfant that his continuance on the project was desirable to the president, reiterating once again that the law required L'Enfant to act in subordination to the Commission. Was L'Enfant willing to continue his services under that condition? In reply, L'Enfant, believing his honor at stake, laid out his grievances against the commissioners. While he very much wished to continue with the project, the commissioners impeded his every effort and he could no longer "act in subjection to their wills and caprice"; if the Residence Act absolutely required that he do so, "I cannot nor would I upon any consideration submit myself to it."[46]

After reading the letter, Washington dispatched Tobias Lear in an attempt to remove what he considered L'Enfant's "unfounded suspicions" about the commissioners. L'Enfant curtly dismissed Lear with the remark "that he had already heard enough of this matter." Washington, who must have lost his usually carefully controlled temper, was still so committed to L'Enfant that he made one final effort to retain his services. Grasping at L'Enfant's straw about interpreting the Residence Act, he called Jefferson, Rep. James Madison—whom he considered "better acquainted with the whole of this matter than any other"—and Attorney General Edmund Randolph to the presidential mansion. Once Randolph made it clear to the president that the law gave no room for interpretation, Washington resigned himself to the inevitable—almost. Now he faced another political quandary. Would L'Enfant raise a public outcry, particularly from the proprietors, most of whom were already angry with the commissioners? More importantly, would the outcry take on a larger dimension by pitting L'Enfant's patron Hamilton against Jefferson who did not like the plan? While he could not control L'Enfant, Washington was a master politician and he knew immediately what to do with his rival cabinet secretaries. Jefferson as secretary of state had drafted Washington's previous letters to L'Enfant, but this time the president asked Hamilton to draft a letter for Jefferson to sign and send. One can still find the draft in Hamilton's handwriting among Jefferson's Papers.

Even then, at the final moment, the fateful letter of 27 February 1792 that led to L'Enfant's resignation gave him an out. Perhaps in concluding that "you absolutely decline acting under the authority of the present commissioners," the president had misunderstood both the planner's letter and his remarks to Lear. L'Enfant replied immediately and directly to Washington. The president had not misunderstood, he could not subordinate himself to the Commission. L'Enfant had resigned. He was not dismissed. Both Jefferson and Washington also understood it that way and so should history. The next day, after unsuccessfully seeking support from Jefferson for having L'Enfant complete preparation of his plan for the engraver, the president wrote L'Enfant, accepting "your final resolution." This time Washington drafted the letter himself and, while assuring L'Enfant "as I have often done" of his desire to keep the planner's services, most of it pointed out how L'Enfant's behavior had hurt the federal city. Nevertheless, the president struck from the draft an opinion he could not bring himself to include—that it would have done no good to change the commissioners because it was feared that L'Enfant would not consent "to be under the control of anyone."[47]

A week after L'Enfant resigned, Washington received a lengthy letter from Commissioner Stuart filled with complaints against the planner that concluded with the announcement that all three commissioners had decided to resign "rather than be any longer subject to the caprices and malicious suggestions of Major L'Enfant." An alternative might be to allow the planner to act independently of the Commission but if that happened, Stuart believed, "the treasury of the Union will not be adequate to the expenses incurred." Stuart took the opportunity to call for a major alteration to L'Enfant's plan. He and others believed that the ground around the president's house was much too extensive; it "may suit the genius of a despotic government to cultivate an immense and gloomy wilderness in the midst of a thriving city" but not the United States. At the same time Commissioner Johnson wrote Jefferson to express several reservations about the plan, especially the diagonal avenues and the extraordinary size of the Capitol. Clearly the Commission did not support L'Enfant's plan.[48]

Jefferson and Washington acted quickly to crush the mounting political disaster. The commissioners were easily mollified since L'Enfant was gone. In sending that news, Jefferson assured them that there had never been a moment's doubt that the president would part with L'Enfant before parting with any one of them. At the same time, Washington sent a private letter to Stuart that defended the size of L'Enfant's presidential square and urged that he be adequately compensated not only because the plan had "met universal applause" but also because L'Enfant had "become a very discontented man." Washington suggested $2,300 and a city lot; the commissioners, in a rare break with their master, offered half that amount and the lot. L'Enfant of course refused the offer.[49]

Soothing the proprietors was another matter. Jefferson sent them the news through Walker, from whom he sought support: "I think you have seen enough of" L'Enfant's "temper to satisfy yourself that he never could have acted under any control, not even that of the President himself." L'Enfant also addressed the proprietors, explaining "the circumstances forcing me now to resign." It was again a matter of honor. He expressed his continued desire for the success of the federal city "hoping that the sentiments by which I have been actuated will secure me that share of merit with you and the public, which the endeavors I have made to promote its true interest may merit." The proprietors, who saw L'Enfant's "extravagant plans, added to his great confidence, and mad zeal" as the map to their future wealth—as his letter to them more than once implied—were incensed by what they considered a forced resignation. With the notable exception of Daniel Carroll of Duddington, who had lost his house, and his relative Notley Young, whose also trespassing house L'Enfant had chosen not to tear down, the proprietors turned to Walker to convince the president to reinstate L'Enfant. They had formed "the highest opinion of his talents, his unwearied Zeal, his firmness (tho sometimes perhaps improperly exerted, in general highly useful), his impartiality to this or that end of the city … and his total disregard of all pecuniary considerations." Walker sent their appeal to the secretary of state with the pointed comment that he feared "the affairs of the City will come into public investigation" if the planner was not reinstated. In reply, Jefferson reminded Walker that "the retirement of Major L'Enfant had been his own act" and suggested that "nobody knows better than yourself the patience and condescensions the President used in order to induce him to continue." The letter soothed the proprietors to the extent that they recognized that L'Enfant could not be independent of the commissioners; nevertheless, they still wanted him back on the job.[50]

The same proprietors also wrote L'Enfant, expressing to him their great respect "for we well know that your time, and the whole powers of your whole mind, have been for many months entirely devoted to the arrangements in the city, which reflect so much honor on your taste and judgment." Washington's fear that L'Enfant might stir up trouble proved unfounded. It was L'Enfant, and not Washington or Jefferson, who finally ended the crisis. In a letter to Walker on 1 April 1791 L'Enfant acknowledged the flattering testimony of the proprietors, but stated unequivocally that nothing could induce him to engage "anew in the business."[51]

L'Enfant made almost a clean break with his grand city on the Potomac during the 1790s. He passed through the area only once when he made an extended trip to Virginia sometime after 1794, visiting with proprietor Samuel Davidson and surely, if he was there, George Walker, with whom L'Enfant continued to correspond throughout the decade. In 1794 proprietor David Burnes conveyed to the planner the gratitude he felt "in his breast" for what L'Enfant had accomplished at Washington. A year later, L'Enfant received a letter from his friend John Trumbull. Expressing his desire "that the noble Plans you had formed" at Washington "might not be entirely defaced by the want of professional knowledge," the letter introduced architect George Hadfield, the brother of Jefferson's dear friend Maria Cosway and the man who had been appointed superintendent of the Capitol. Trumbull had told Hadfield that L'Enfant was probably the only person in the United States with as much architectural knowledge as Hadfield.

L'Enfant had only one official contact with the federal city after 1792, and that was on behalf of Isaac Roberdeau, the faithful assistant with whom he had lived at Georgetown in 1791. In June 1795, immediately after the last of the three original commissioners resigned, Roberdeau sent a letter to the Commission about his unpaid claim for expenses in 1791 and 1792. In a private reply, William Thornton, the amateur architect who had won the design competition for the Capitol and one of the recently appointed commissioners, suggested that Roberdeau seek written verification of his claim from L'Enfant. Thornton took the opportunity to ask what L'Enfant would consider as compensation "for the great exertion[s of his?] genius and talents." Roberdeau carried the letter to his former supervisor, who, while not responding to the question about his own compensation, sent a letter to the Commission on behalf of Roberdeau in December that resulted in payment of the claim.[52]

George Washington, on his part, always regretted L'Enfant's loss and never turned his back on the city plan that he so much admired. This

Handkerchief Map

L'Enfant's manuscript plan for the city of Washington, D.C., without his name, is shown here imprinted on a linen handkerchief engraved in Boston by Samuel Hill in 1792. Like Savage's use of the same map in his painting *The Washington Family*, it is evidence of the extent to which the icon's symbolism had permeated the popular consciousness. (Courtesy of the Museum of American History, Smithsonian Institution, Washington, D.C.)

says as much about Washington's character as about his opinion of L'Enfant's genius, for probably no one else ever made him grovel as much as L'Enfant. It is not known whether in time Washington came to see the events of the winter of 1791–92 in a different light, given that Andrew Ellicott, George Hadfield, and many of the other creative individuals who came to work on the federal city had problems with the commissioners similar to L'Enfant's and either quit or were dismissed. Ellicott, who had associated with L'Enfant during his surveys in the District of Columbia, left two vivid descriptions of his colleague. "Though not one of the most handsome of men," the surveyor informed his wife a few months after the men met in 1791, "he is from his good breeding and native politeness a first rate favorite among the ladies." Later he concluded that L'Enfant had a lively imagination and a willingness to make

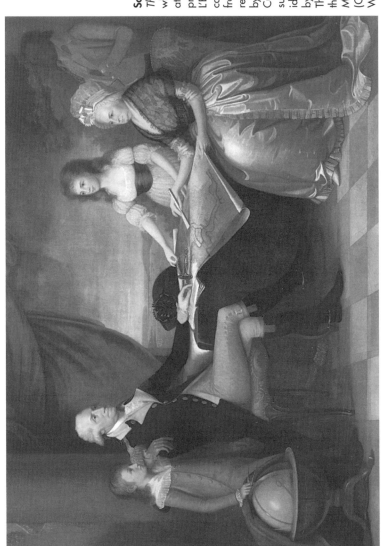

Savage Painting

The Washington Family, the large oil painting which Edward Savage (1761–1817) completed at Philadelphia in 1796, aptly interpreted the president's overriding vision: his arm rests on L'Enfant's map of the city, whose ascendency as capital of the republican empire can be traced from Washington's hand to the shoulders (and responsibility) of a newer generation represented by his step-grandson, George Washington Parke Custis. The position of the boy's hand, in turn, suggests the global dominion of the nation's ideals if not its arms, which may be symbolized by the sword hilt at Washington's left hand. Through the drapery in the background is visible the Potomac River flowing out of the West past Mount Vernon, the imagined locale of the sitting. (Courtesy of the National Gallery of Art, Washington, D.C.)

decisions, but no system for their execution, without which there could be no economy, certainty, or decision.[53]

"A HIGH OPINION OF THE SOLIDITY OF HIS TALENTS"

In January 1792, as the relationship between L'Enfant and the commissioners crumbled, Isaac Roberdeau told an acquaintance that he and L'Enfant would never submit to the Commission; instead they would go to Pennsylvania where "they had offers" and "could be employed when they pleased." One of these was from Pennsylvania Governor Thomas Mifflin who had approached L'Enfant about building a presidential mansion at Philadelphia. Instead, L'Enfant was rescued from unemployment by his friend and patron Alexander Hamilton, the guiding force behind The Society for Establishing Useful Manufactures. The Society hired L'Enfant in August for one year to construct the water works and buildings on its land at Paterson, New Jersey.[54]

Unable to control L'Enfant, the federal city commissioners had turned on Roberdeau in January 1792 and had him arrested for trespass. Two months later as the two parties moved toward an accommodation, Roberdeau, addressing L'Enfant for the first time as "my dear friend" instead of "my dear sir," promised that he would accept no terms dishonorable to either himself or L'Enfant. The planner was just as loyal to his assistant and as soon as the engineer was hired by the Society, he sent Roberdeau to Hamilton with a letter urging that Roberdeau, who had quit working at the federal city "from a regard for me," be hired as his assistant: "I need not mention to you my attachment to him and the consideration which lead [sic] me to retain him near me." Roberdeau expressed his gratitude for the offer and "the pleasure I have in your Society and with what cheerfulness I will do every thing that may expedite your wishes and give you pleasure." But there was a complication, for he was no longer as "uncommitted as when I was with you" at Georgetown. Much to Roberdeau's delight his fiancee indicated that she would be pleased to live at Paterson and looked forward to L'Enfant's company. "I am truly much pleased with the Idea of being with you," Roberdeau concluded.[55]

L'Enfant proposed an aqueduct to carry water from the Passaic River to power the proposed factories at Paterson and presented the Society with a city plan that one newspaper described as far exceeding anything of the kind yet seen in the United States. The superintendent kept Hamilton informed of his progress, repeating a commitment not to be lavish with the Society's funds. And Hamilton who, "from much experience and observation" of L'Enfant had "a high opinion of the solidity of his talents" and believed he would never undertake anything that he was not capable of executing "solidly and well," continued to promote the engineer with the directors. In October, when one of them urged the appointment of iron manufacturer Samuel Ogden to superintend the entire project, Hamilton objected strongly on the grounds that Ogden was "one of the most opinionated men I ever knew" and would surely "drive L'Enfant off the ground." Further, Hamilton pointed out, Ogden had declared that L'Enfant knew nothing of waterworks when in fact it was part of his profession, for he was "what is called in France a *civil Engineer* that is an Artist acquainted with Mechanics generally; particularly in reference to Architecture Aqueducts Canals &c &c including necessarily a knowledge of Hydraulics."[56]

By February 1793 L'Enfant was spending much of his time at Philadelphia rather than Paterson. Things began to seriously fall apart in late March when L'Enfant learned that Ogden intended to make the Society a proposal for delivering the water necessary to power the factories that differed from his own. His professional honor once again at stake, L'Enfant stopped work and discharged the workers until such time as the Society chose between the two of them, expressing to Hamilton his discouragement and fear that his plans would be set aside and that he would "once more" be driven off. Hamilton quickly assured L'Enfant of his support and his opinion that the Society would never approve Ogden's proposal, taking the opportunity however to communicate his displeasure with L'Enfant for dismissing the workers without the direction of the Board of Directors.

At its April meeting the Board, seriously alarmed at L'Enfant's extensive plans, ordered that he confine his entire attention to completion of the aqueduct. Peter Colt, superintendent of the factories (and later famous for his revolver), doubted the mortified L'Enfant's ability to accommodate his plans to the Society's funds. He urged Hamilton to impress on the engineer once again the importance of the greatest economy and of "confining his views to those things which are essential instead of what is ornamental." In June, a committee of the Board notified L'Enfant that all the operations with which he was involved should cease because it was certain that its funds were altogether inadequate to support his plans. L'Enfant returned to Philadelphia apparently without turning over a copy of his town plan and both parties agreed that his year long contract would not be renewed. For a second time, L'Enfant's grand plans and an inability to accommodate to the needs of his employers had cost him a project. When the Society did not pay him what he believed he was owed, L'Enfant turned to Hamilton, demanding that he resolve the matter on the grounds that he was responsible for getting L'Enfant involved.[57]

Another factor contributing to the failure at Paterson was the fact that a new project had captured the architect's imagination. In May Robert Morris had complained to him that, while he had previously thought he would have to give up his dream mansion because of want of money, he now feared he would have to give it up for want of L'Enfant.

"Morris's Folly"

This engraving is the only image of a residence known to have been designed by L'Enfant. It appeared in *Views of Philadelphia* (Philadelphia, 1800), a work superintended by the artist William Birch (1755–1834) and illustrated by his son Thomas (1779–1851). The book's highly selective engravings portray the sights Birch conceived as best glorifying Philadelphia's prosperity at the end of its ten-year stint as the seat of federal government. Although Birch labeled the plate "An Unfinished House in Chestnut Street," it is traditionally identified as "Morris's Folly" because of its three principal features: its unusual roof design; its size and extravagance; and—most vividly—the surrounding evidence of the never ending construction that eventually gave L'Enfant's most important private commission its derisive name. The Birches' view shows the project three years after L'Enfant abandoned it and one year before it was demolished. (Courtesy of the Public Library of Philadelphia)

Robert Morris
Robert Morris (1735–1806) was already an influential patron of the arts before he hired L'Enfant to design a Philadelphia mansion for him. This portrait by Robert Edge Pine (1730?–1788) shows Morris around 1785—not long after his resignation as superintendent of finance, the most important executive officer of the Confederation government. Like L'Enfant, Pine had a complex financial relationship with Morris. In 1786 the "financier of the Revolution" appears to have loaned Pine the money to build his own home, studio and gallery not far from the site of "Morris's Folly"—perhaps a partial reward for this portrait, said to be Mrs. Mary Morris's favorite. (Robert G. Stewart, *Robert Edge Pine: A British Portrait Painter in America, 1784–1788* [Washington, D.C., 1979], pp. 25, 69–71) (Courtesy of the National Portrait Gallery, Smithsonian Institution, Washington, D.C.)

"This note pursuant to previous invitation," L'Enfant later claimed, "caused me to quit the Paterson business." Over the decade since resigning as Congress's superintendent of finance, Morris had made a fortune in the China trade and by 1793 he was anxious to build the largest house in Philadelphia to reflect that wealth. Like Hamilton, Morris had great respect for L'Enfant's talents, believing he deserved high credit for his plan of Washington and that the commissioners ought never to have parted with his services. To L'Enfant the Morris commission must have been a dream for, unlike the supervisors of the Washington and Paterson projects, the good natured Morris let the architect have his way and provided all the needed money.

On the square between Chestnut, Walnut, Seventh and Eighth streets, L'Enfant designed and constructed a huge multi-sided, lavish brick mansion with pale blue marble window frames and porticoes and a mansard roof that he covered with large iron sheets, probably the first time such a method of construction was employed in the United States. By September 1795 Morris had become frustrated with the architect's progress. The mansion was not yet roofed as promised and "uncalled for" remarks in response to his complaint led Morris, who rightly maintained that he was incapable of doing injustice to the architect's reputation, to declare L'Enfant's excuse "more ingenious than just." Morris also suggested that if L'Enfant did not think that, as the client, he had a right to obtain satisfaction from the architect "we should part." A year later Morris was astonished to see that L'Enfant had pulled down the work of the year before in order to put up more marble when Morris had originally only agreed to include any marble as an indulgence of the architect's genius. Morris accused L'Enfant of exposing him to ridicule and such increasing costs—already greater than the architect's estimates—that Morris would have to abandon the house. L'Enfant's explanation soothed his amiable client and the project continued.[58]

The professional relationship between the two men was complicated by the fact that they became otherwise financially involved during the project. L'Enfant purchased five shares in Morris's North American Land Company and loaned the merchant his twelve shares of Bank of the United States stock. When in 1797 L'Enfant demanded the bank stock back, Morris could not satisfy the demand, strapped as he was from the cost of the mansion and rapidly falling into bankruptcy because of overextended land speculation in Washington, D.C., western New York, and throughout the southern states that totaled more than six million acres. Morris lamented that they were both in the same situation and promised that L'Enfant was constantly on his mind. When he was imprisoned for debt in February 1798, Morris, suffering "the greatest anxiety" because he knew the "disinterested" loan had caused L'Enfant real hardship, placed a lien in L'Enfant's name on some of the stock in his Genesee tract in western New York as compensation for the bank stock loan. The architect stopped work on the mansion in 1797 and never submitted a final bill to Morris. "Morris's Folly," as it had become known, was demolished in 1801, the same year Morris was released from prison.[59]

While engaged on Morris's house L'Enfant had taken on another project for the federal government. In March 1794, Congress finally appropriated money for the defense of American ports, something L'Enfant had been advocating for a decade. Secretary of War Henry

Knox, with the explicit approval of President Washington, appointed the engineer to fortify Wilmington, Delaware, and Philadelphia. By July L'Enfant's plans had alarmed powerful voices in Philadelphia's merchant community and soon thereafter state and federal officials in both Delaware and Pennsylvania. The latter state launched a legislative investigation, the only time L'Enfant's work was subjected to this type of scrutiny. His sense of honor took offense at what he considered all the "misrepresentations of the motives actuating me" and L'Enfant quit the project during the winter of 1794–1795.[60]

"ALL HE HAS DONE FOR ME WAS NOT CHARITY"

When L'Enfant returned to Philadelphia in 1793 he resided in the same boarding house as Richard Soderstrom, a fellow former European aristocrat whom he had met in New York City in 1786 or 1787 and to whom he began loaning money "the very first day, that is the very next morning of the day" they met. By the end of the 1790s the two became deeply entwined emotionally and financially and Soderstrom controlled L'Enfant's mind and money. The proud and trusting L'Enfant had allowed himself to become an impoverished, servantless, dependent Cinderella, keeping to himself in two sparsely furnished, cold, dark rooms in the large house at the corner of Filbert and 8th Streets for which they had agreed, in June 1794, to share the rent. (The city directories indicate that L'Enfant considered himself "engineer of the United States" and that his friend Isaac Roberdeau lived nearby.)

Soderstrom and L'Enfant ended their relationship in 1804 when Soderstrom filed suit against L'Enfant in federal court. Soderstrom sought $7,300, arguing that their pre-moving in together arrangement made L'Enfant responsible for half their living expenses, not just half the rent for the six years and eight months they had lived together in Philadelphia. Reflecting on the relationship, while defending himself against the suit, L'Enfant depicted himself in the deeply hurt, resentful language of a powerless, subordinate martyr whose honor as a gentleman had been degraded. He clearly regretted that he had taken to heart Soderstrom's repeated admonition not to worry about their informal exchange of money, burning all of Soderstrom's promissory notes only to learn from the suit that Soderstrom had kept all of L'Enfant's receipts. Disgusted at being called on to pay half the wages and food of the many servants Soderstrom maintained to support his high lifestyle, L'Enfant wondered that Soderstrom had not "charged me with his horse food & for the expenses of the number of Harlots of his Friends."[61]

Richard Soderstrom is one of those many elusive figures of whom greater knowledge would enrich the landscape of early American history. A member of a wealthy and influential merchant family from Gothenburg, Sweden, Soderstrom established himself as a merchant at

Henry Knox
Henry Knox (1750–1806) was an important patron to L'Enfant while serving as secretary of war from 1785 to 1795. Their careers intersected at many points: Knox's
artillery regiments worked in close collaboration with the corps of engineers; Knox
served as first secretary general of The Society of the Cincinnati; and each became
an advisor to George Washington on matters close to the president's heart: the
regulation of the federal army and the creation of an appropriate federal capital.
Constantino Brumidi (1805–80) painted this oil on plaster (a technique known as
fresco in scialbatura) for the President's Room of the Capitol in 1859–60.
(Courtesy of the Office of the Architect of the Capitol)

Boston sometime after King Gustavus III issued him a passport in
October 1781. He shipped rice, tobacco and other products to Europe,
quickly winning the respect of the Boston elite. Five months after the
United States concluded one of its earliest treaties of peace and

commerce with Sweden in April 1783, Soderstrom received a royal commission as consul to represent Swedish interests in the northern states. As such he traveled frequently between Boston and New York City, where he had an address as early as 1783, conducted private commercial business, and consulted Alexander Hamilton about representing him in a lawsuit.[62] Soderstrom went to Trenton in November 1784 to present his diplomatic credentials to the Confederation Congress, but left without achieving his purpose when no quorum formed. Soderstrom's involvement with Congress was far from over however, for he became the focus of an early state-federal controversy as the infant federal government struggled to maintain and assert its severely limited prerogatives.

The influential New York merchant Isaac Sears and his partner endorsed approximately $30,000 in bills of exchange on Soderstrom's brother in Sweden (merchants Clement Biddle of Philadelphia and Thomas Russell of Boston endorsed another approximately $20,000). In January 1785, after Richard Soderstrom had refused to honor some of the bills, his New York creditors tried to have him arrested one Saturday night in Boston. The sheriff could not locate him. On the following Monday afternoon Governor John Hancock officially recognized Soderstrom's commission as Swedish consul, thus granting him diplomatic immunity. When the New York firm complained to Congress, Secretary for Foreign Affairs John Jay and Congress rightly insisted that Massachusetts had acted in violation of the Articles of Confederation, which placed foreign affairs solely in the hands of Congress. Jay urged Congress to inform the Swedish government about "the disrespectful and unprecedented manner" in which Soderstrom had entered on the execution of his commission, and to request that "he may be forthwith dismissed, with such Marks of his Majesty's displeasure, as might discountenance the like Liberties in future."

Boston's elite flooded the Massachusetts congressional delegation with letters in support of Soderstrom's character—"remarkably modest and unassuming," "most honorable, amiable, and manly," one who "would scorn an advantage that reflected on his honor." More importantly, the letters, particularly ones from the creditor firm's agent and attorney in Boston, proved not only that Soderstrom had not sought diplomatic immunity to escape jail but also that he had been arrested and quickly bailed by the wealthy and influential Thomas Russell. Congress recognized Soderstrom's commission in May 1785, with Jay asserting to a Bostonian that his severity about the matter had been entirely because of his duty to protect the interests of the federal government. When the consul came to New York and demanded that Congress give him a copy of the complaint, Congress saved some face by refusing. Soderstrom continued to do business in New York, and diplomatic immunity did not save him in 1790 from having all of his property confiscated and spending time behind "the grates" of its debtor prison, where both L'Enfant and the Dutch Ambassador came to his assistance.[63]

In 1795 Soderstrom became Consul General for Sweden in the United States and as such began appointing vice consuls. By 1810 at least sixteen men had received the appointments, including a Jonathan Swift in the District of Columbia—four years before Congress assumed jurisdiction there separate from Maryland and Virginia. How much money Soderstrom made from selling these appointments is unrecorded. During the 1790s Soderstrom also served as a commercial agent for Denmark and represented the interests of both nations with the federal government. In that capacity he shipped bundles of American newspapers to both, charging half of the cost to L'Enfant. Privately he became involved with Robert Morris, selling North American Land Company stock and convincing L'Enfant to loan Morris his bank stock. Acting as L'Enfant's financial agent he collected $3,000 from Morris to pay L'Enfant for work on Morris's mansion, keeping much of it for himself according to L'Enfant. Known as a lavish entertainer in Philadelphia diplomatic and social circles, Soderstrom was probably widely admired for what he portrayed as his charitable assistance to L'Enfant. A man almost obsessed with honor, L'Enfant found this highly offensive—"all he has done for me was not charity."[64]

Having lost the Morris commission and desperately in need of money in the summer of 1798, L'Enfant decided to approach Alexander Hamilton about compensation from New York City for his work on Federal Hall. The architect, who had often spent the winter months in New York during the 1790s, later claimed to be too impoverished to make the trip to New York. Soderstrom volunteered to undertake the business. When he returned he reported remarks Hamilton had made about L'Enfant's conduct in his previous employments and about his relationship with the French Ambassador at Philadelphia. L'Enfant considered his honor assaulted as a veteran, as a professional and as a servant of America. The proud man, humiliated by his dependence on Soderstrom even if he had not yet acknowledged it to himself, initiated an affair of honor against Hamilton, the man who more than any other had been his friend, patron and protector.

The first step of such an affair was a letter demanding that a gentleman either confirm or deny an alleged comment or action. Failure to respond at all led to public disgrace. Failure to respond satisfactorily could lead to a duel. L'Enfant's letter demanded to know why his political principles and professional conduct had become matters for Hamilton's comment. A skilled veteran of such affairs of honor, Hamilton, who was involved in at least a dozen before he died as a result of one, was stunned by the letter and replied immediately, taking great care with his words. He had indeed said that L'Enfant's political opinions were supportive of revolutionary France, that such a closeness existed between L'Enfant and the French Ambassador that it was assumed L'Enfant was in the pay of the French government, and that consequently L'Enfant could not expect any employment with the United States. Hamilton however asserted that these were not his opinions but ones that had come from elsewhere. L'Enfant accepted the formulaic explanation, but expressed amazement that, after having been "amongst the first who have fought and bled for the attainment of American liberty and Independence," a mere good wish for France would banish him from employment. He demanded to know from whom Hamilton had heard the opinions; whether Hamilton replied is unknown, and, like most affairs of honor, the incident ended short of pistols. L'Enfant's French sympathies had been surely exaggerated, for soon after the affair he sought a commission in the American army during the quasi-war with France. The fact that his letter of application was written from New York in November 1798 suggests that his lack of money was also exaggerated.[65]

"A PITIFUL DIRTY FELLOW … THE PICTURE OF FAMINE"

L'Enfant's life changed again dramatically in December 1799 when the death of George Washington freed him from a self-imposed moratorium on any claim on the federal government for his services in designing the federal city. In late September 1800, Soderstrom and L'Enfant joined the exodus of the federal government from Philadelphia and took up residence at Stelly and Barney's Tavern in the City of Washington. At the end of a day of lobbying at the Capitol on behalf of the petition that L'Enfant had submitted to the lame duck Federalist Congress and about to return to Philadelphia on business, Soderstrom wrote L'Enfant a letter of advice. All of the congressmen Soderstrom had spoken with considered the too lengthy petition filled with generalizations rather than facts and figures. L'Enfant should submit another, shorter and specific, stating how much salary he wanted per day and how much his expenses had been. Further, Soderstrom instructed, do not depend on "General [Henry] Lee or your own [Federalist] party …. If I should tell you what the[y] say of your writing you would take care of writing such long memorials again." Not to follow his advice, Soderstrom warned, would mean that L'Enfant would leave town without getting anything.[66]

L'Enfant could not afford to leave, and he spent the remainder of his life in and about Washington petitioning Congress to settle his claim while pursuing others of less magnitude. Incapable of conciseness when he perceived his honor and reputation at stake, L'Enfant's frequent, lengthy petitions are evidence that he did not follow all of Soderstrom's advice. This was fortunate for posterity because the petitions over the course of the next quarter of a century are rich with detail and insight waiting to be deciphered. They contain information about his visionary plan for "a splendid inviting Capital," about the amount of his own money that he spent in the endeavor, and about the events of 1791 and their aftermath. In addition, they join his memorial of 1784 calling on the Confederation Congress to create an army corps of engineers as the primary sources for L'Enfant's advanced ideas about the quality of urban life, the funding of large scale public construction projects, the role of the federal government in American society, and the professions of architecture, engineering and city planning.[67]

In his second petition in January 1801, L'Enfant took Soderstrom's advice to be specific about money: for his labor, $8,000; for lost profit from the sale of copies of his plan, $37,500; and for "enterprise," by which the planner meant creativity, $50,000. Later that year he put his case before President Thomas Jefferson to whom he did not feel the necessity of detailing the events of 1791–92. Instead he focused on his volunteer services to the United States over the course of twenty-five years, his wounds at Savannah, his captivity at Charleston, and his mission to France for The Society of the Cincinnati that he had undertaken at great personal cost and that had so embarrassed his financial well being. The "only reproach to which I may be liable is being more attached to principle than ambitious of raising myself, too zealous for public Interests," and too dependent "on mouth made promises." Jefferson did not respond and L'Enfant sent a second letter in March 1802 expressing apprehension about the silence. The president replied immediately with the devastating news that he had forwarded the earlier letter to the federal city commissioners, the only duly constituted authority.[68]

The City of Washington that L'Enfant inhabited—some would say haunted—was not the city he had designed. More was buried than just the body of a man when George Washington was laid to rest in 1799 and Thomas Jefferson was elected president in the so-called Revolution of 1800. The great commercial American seat of empire on the Potomac River that Washington, L'Enfant and George Walker envisioned died as well. Thomas Jefferson and the Democratic Republican Party he led saw to it that the dream was not realized. The American diplomat William Short was not alone when he complained to Jefferson in 1795 about the "great and irreparable defects which experience will show" in L'Enfant's plan. Indeed, the city became an issue in the highly charged paranoid politics of the late 1790s. To Democratic Republicans it symbolized as little else could the high-toned grandeur and expensive, centralizing, anti-democratic, repressive policies that they associated with such Federalist enemies as incumbent President John Adams. Adams's eloquent remarks about the "capital" when he addressed Congress at its first session in Washington in 1800 were not echoed by Thomas Jefferson in his inaugural address to Congress soon thereafter. Indeed Jefferson did not mention the new seat of government at all.[69]

Thomas Jefferson wanted a federal town, not a federal city, which he saw as anti-republican and a threat to the states as well as a reflection of Europe's aristocratic cities. Indeed, he liked the natural setting and rural charm of Washington and refused to support any appropriations to implement the original plan except for the completion of the public buildings and the improvement of Pennsylvania Avenue between the Capitol and the White House, as it was soon to be known. His dream for the city was perhaps best expressed by a contemporary: "Washington will, for a long time, have a moral advantage over other great cities," concluded David Bailie Warden, American consul at Paris, "as the sublime scenery of a majestic river, beautified by the luxuriant hangings of woods, rocks, and meadows, keep alive in the breasts of the beholders the native feelings of truth and nature, and prevent their minds from being corrupted by the artificial lures of emasculated softness and gregarious vices."[70]

The decade following 1800 was the worst of L'Enfant's life, particularly after May 1804 when Soderstrom stopped supporting him and L'Enfant signed over to the Swede the lot he had purchased in 1791 and the value of his claim on Congress for the design of the federal city. More than once during those years he was subject to lawsuit, almost penniless and homeless. In 1803 L'Enfant's good friend from their days together in Georgetown, proprietor Samuel Davidson, gave up on L'Enfant's ten year old debt for $45, on the grounds that the city planner was now "a pitiful dirty fellow and very poor." Three years later Architect of the Capitol Benjamin H. Latrobe limned a stark image for posterity: "daily through the city stalks the picture of famine, L'Enfant and his dog.... [he] had the courage to undertake any public work whatever that was offered to him. He has not succeeded in any, but was always honest and is now miserably poor." These assessments modify somewhat banker and patron of the arts William W. Corcoran's oft-repeated, but hearsay, description of the planner at this time as "a tall, thin man, fully six feet in height, finely proportioned, nose prominent, of military bearing, courtly air, and polite manners, his figure usually enveloped in a long overcoat and surmounted by a bell-crowned hat—a man who would attract attention in any assembly." Fortunately we have Corcoran's own observation that the L'Enfant he remembered from his childhood "was very poor and very proud," "a great pedestrian" who often came to Georgetown where he had many "friends and admirers," including Corcoran's father the mayor, to whom L'Enfant gave advice about the construction of a stone causeway from Virginia to Analostan (now Roosevelt) Island in 1810.[71]

While focused on his claim before Congress, L'Enfant was not unmindful of other avenues that he might pursue for the money he so desperately needed. In January 1801 he again sought payment for Federal Hall. The ten acres he had been awarded a decade earlier had since been platted into lots and sold by the city for approximately $1,500. Robert

Morris kindly lent his assistance and that of his attorney son Thomas, a member of Congress from New York City. Based on the reaction of the New York City Council to a petition from L'Enfant, Thomas Morris was certain that the matter would be resolved to the architect's satisfaction, the only thing in dispute being whether to give him the entire $1,500. The Council decided on half that amount and L'Enfant refused the settlement, unsuccessfully requesting the city to reconsider. Thomas Morris had some difficulty in getting Hamilton to use his considerable influence on behalf of "poor L'Enfant," information that Robert Morris passed on to L'Enfant in writing. L'Enfant was outraged and demanded an explanation from Hamilton. Whether the letter, in which he expressed his thoughts "freely" and "openly," was written in the formulaic language of an affair of honor cannot be known as neither it nor Hamilton's response survives, a situation not unusual in Hamilton's carefully sanitized papers but uncommon in L'Enfant's.

Hamilton's reply elicited an acknowledgment of all that he had done for L'Enfant over the years, and the architect apologized, at least by implication: "let those ideas and expressions as I may have introduced in a disagreeable way, be passed over as having no meaning respecting to yourself." His misapprehensions about Hamilton were "owing no doubt to the taint of matters engaging my mind at the time." Once again he insisted that he was certain that neither in a civil or military capacity nor in private conversation had he committed any act or even expressed any sentiment that did not certify his good faith and his "earnest solicitude and zeal for the glory as well as interest of the United States!" He remained in Washington primarily to obtain his just due from Congress, but also because of his poverty, and "the impossibility of living elsewhere in the obscure private way I do." He did not believe that the congressional claim would be settled quickly and his only hope for relief was a settlement with New York City, of which "having the promise of your hearty and personal exertions in my behalf, I remain confident of success." Two days later he sent a second letter, informing Hamilton that he had sent congratulations to the new mayor of New York and used the opportunity to call attention to his claim and suggest that the mayor obtain the particulars from Hamilton.[72] It is the last we hear of the Federal Hall claim for twenty years. This was perhaps because Aaron Burr, not Peter L'Enfant, mortally wounded Alexander Hamilton in a duel on 11 July 1804.

When faced in August 1801 with what he conceived as a refusal of assistance on Hamilton's part, L'Enfant turned to another possible source of relief—compensation for the fortification project on the Delaware River in 1794. Appealing to the sympathy of former Secretary of War Henry Knox, he laid out the embarrassing details of his situation and asked Knox for verification of his employment since the documents had perished in the November 1800 war department fire at Washington. Knox wrote Secretary of War Henry Dearborn on behalf of L'Enfant whom he described as "an old soldier whose inattention to money matters is as well known to his acquaintances as the excellency of his talents as an engineer." By the spring of 1802 L'Enfant was appealing to Dearborn for immediate relief because he was for the first time in his life subject to a court order issued against him and, at the same time, subject to arrest for want of a few weeks room and board. In July 1805, the secretary urged an assistant to attempt to settle the matter expeditiously on the ground that the claimant "appears to be poor and in real distress."[73]

Desperate, in 1802 L'Enfant sought to recoup the value of his loaned bank stock from Robert Morris. Once again Morris indicated his heartfelt concern, explaining the frustrations he had experienced in trying to obtain money for L'Enfant, and encouraging him to pursue his claims on New York City and Congress. Having said that, he also told the architect that he should have omitted the first part of his letter, for "reproaches heaped on the unfortunate inflict incurable wounds without drawing benefit to the maker." When Morris died in 1806, L'Enfant refused to add his name to those making claims on the estate, an act considered so honorable that it found a place in L'Enfant's own obituary. In 1807 the still desperate L'Enfant recalled the land in Ohio that the United States had granted him for his service during the Revolutionary War and attempted to learn how much it was worth and how much had been sold for unpaid taxes.[74]

The situation came to a head in 1808 when the owner of Rhodes Tavern at 15th Street and Pennsylvania Avenue threatened to kick L'Enfant out for non payment of a $300 tab. In 1804 Congress had authorized the superintendent of the City of Washington to settle with L'Enfant. Negotiations proved fruitless because the two parties were tens of thousands of dollars apart. Faced in 1808 with the choice of settling with the federal government or homelessness, L'Enfant settled for $4,600 and the lot offered to him by the Commission in 1792. But there was a stipulation. Soderstrom had won his suit against L'Enfant in June 1806 and placed a lien on L'Enfant's claim. The Swedish Consul General took just over $4,000 of the settlement; his attorney took the promised city lot; and the city planner received $448.13, most of which probably went to William Rhodes. L'Enfant may have been able to keep the change—unless other creditors managed to get it from him. Seven years later Soderstrom died, still a Swedish subject and living a comfortable life in Philadelphia.[75]

"WE LOVE HIM & HE DESERVES IT FOR HE LOVES US TENDERLY"

Even for its time, L'Enfant's life was unusually male-centric. Given his closeness to Isaac Roberdeau and in particular the emotional intensity of his defense against Richard Soderstrom's suit, readers may wonder if any of L'Enfant's relationships with men had a sexual expression. While the terms "homosexual" and "heterosexual" did not exist until the late nineteenth century, sexual activity among people of the same gender, and awareness of it, did. Because sexuality had not yet acquired the personal and cultural emphasis that it gained in the twentieth century, it was not often the subject of the written discourses upon which historians rely, the exception being political attacks such as those suffered by Alexander Hamilton and Thomas Jefferson. Consequently we will probably never have smoking-gun proof as to whether any of L'Enfant's relationships with men had a sexual component. And, if they did, that fact in no way disputes the claim that while he was living with Richard Soderstrom in 1797, L'Enfant fathered a child named Mary, mother unknown.

Before classification of people into sexual categories, intense emotional friendships like that between L'Enfant and Soderstrom could exist between men, independent of their marital status, without people assuming anything about sexuality, even when they lived alone together. When apart, such friends often expressed devotion and love as well as the anguish of separation; if the friendship was cross generational, its expression often employed a father-son frame of reference. Historians confronted by these love letters have almost invariably veiled their significance with a dismissive and factually incorrect remark about "the flowery language of the times." Several examples of such friendships survive from the Early American Republic. Charles Nourse, son of Register of the Treasury Joseph Nourse, became so attached to the Georgetown merchant Frederick Delius that he followed him to Europe. Two hours before being blown up in Tripoli Harbor in 1804, Captain Richard Somers gave fellow naval hero and soon-to-be inconsolable Captain Stephen Decatur a gold ring engraved "Tripoli 1804" on the outside and "R.S. to S. D. 1804" on the inside. The intense long term relationship between the poet Joel Barlow and the inventor Robert Fulton on the Left Bank in Paris and at Kalorama on the border of the City of Washington included a third person, Barlow's wife Ruth.[76]

Many of the documented male friendships of the early republic were between men who had bonded in the Continental Army. Unwilling to be separated, the American Major George Schaffner joined General Charles Armand-Tuffin when he returned to France at the end of the war. Better known are the relationships between George Washington and the Marquis de Lafayette and between Washington's military aides and L'Enfant's friends and patrons Alexander Hamilton and John Laurens. Frederick Steuben's relationship with Peter Stephen DuPonceau, to whom he had first been attracted at a party in Paris in 1777, was not as close after the War as it had been during his service as Steuben's aide. Nevertheless, fifty years later DuPonceau recalled it with affection: Steuben "watched over me with a father's care" and once said "if you write in the news-papers or get married I will renounce you."

DuPonceau, who took the oath of allegiance to United States in October 1781, went on to do both these things and to become America's preeminent international lawyer and philologist.[77]

Less well known, but by far the most expressive and best documented, is the friendship among three other of L'Enfant's friends, Frederick Steuben and his two former military aides, William North and Benjamin Walker.[78] After the War, Steuben, like L'Enfant, anglicized his name and settled in New York City where Billy North and Ben Walker lived. North stood at the center of the triad, comfortably expressing his love to both "the Baron" and Ben while at the same time struggling to understand the meaning of the friendship: "the common acceptation of the word friendship, means scarcely more than acquaintance, or at the most relationship, but friendship, such as I feel for You [Walker] the Baron & *one* or *two* more binds us more closely to each other than any other tye."[79] Of the Baron, he observed to Ben, "We love him & he deserves it for he loves us tenderly."[80]

North believed that the three of them should live together and that his and Walker's wives should submit to that situation. Mary "Polly" North found the relationship among the men somewhat straining and she could not be prevailed on to name a son after Ben. Steuben thought that both Billy's and Ben's wives needed to know that they were only wives and not mistresses. Soon after Steuben advised Billy that he lived under too severe a petticoat government, Mary, in Billy's presence, told the Baron that all his plans were "castles in the air." This sent Billy into a stomping rage at the dinner table, waking their son Frederick, the Baron's namesake. From Steuben's point of view his "Dear Billy" was so important that, when listing for him the memorable events that had occurred on his own birth date, 17 September, Steuben added to the signing of the Constitution and Burgoyne's surrender at Saratoga, that it was the date North had carved their names into a tree. Walker was less expressive of his feelings than either Steuben or North, but his wife too often found herself at "cross purposes" with Steuben whom she called an "Old Savage."[81] By his will Steuben made Billy and Ben his "adopted children" and heirs. The dozens of letters exchanged among the three await their Boswell.

"MY OLD CHUM MAJOR"

A year before he was forced by impending homelessness to settle with the federal government in 1808, L'Enfant submitted a third petition to Congress. It resulted in a bill signed by President James Madison in May 1810 awarding the city planner $666.66 with interest from 1792. Needless to say, L'Enfant considered the sum paltry but once again there was no choice but to take the approximately $1,400. Surely it was owed to somebody. And just as surely there would be a fourth petition as L'Enfant sought a settlement closer to the $95,000 to which he envisioned himself entitled. Perhaps hoping to bring closure to the twenty year old claim and at the same time provide the now fifty-eight year old Revolutionary War hero with the kind of special honor to which he thought himself entitled, Madison made L'Enfant an unsolicited offer. On 7 July 1812 Secretary of War William Eustis officially informed Peter Charles L'Enfant of his appointment as Professor of the Art of Engineering at West Point.

L'Enfant was shocked by what he considered an unexpected mark of esteem from Madison, who was not only close to Jefferson but also not part of the cadre of Continental Army officer friends that had looked after his interests for thirty years. Rejoicing at the opportunity to be restored "to a life of useful activity" from a life "which has thrown me down so helpless in the mire," he seriously reflected on the state of his affairs before informing Eustis that he could not accept the appointment. From his "terrifying" reflections over the course of ten days, out poured a pained rendition of his situation, focused on the suppression of his name from the record as the original projector of the plan of the City of Washington. His only hope for vindication and a just reward was his claim before Congress. Consequently he did not want to be sent to a *"confinement more dismal,"* at a distance where the claim would be harder to advocate and where he might be arrested for debts that were far greater than he could repay out of twenty years salary in any public office.

More to the point, L'Enfant did not think he had the qualities of an instructor. Besides difficulties with English and a memory that did not retain technical terms, he was "not fond of youth": "I am adverse to the society of those self important talkative temperament[s] whose vanity for what little they remember from the reading of works, make them talk at random about every subject and on matter[s] and thing[s] which they often do not understand and which so frequently make fools be mistaken for genius." Nor did he have reverence for "modern academicians." As to West Point itself, he did not support its mission as he had often said publicly and privately. Americans should not "make a pageant of imitation" of the institutions of other nations: American military education should occur in the field in peace time as well as during war. Also, since the law forbade Academy staff from an active command in the army, he would be denied participation "in the danger" and the "glory of the field of action which is now opening!" between England and the United States. Finally, at West Point he would be subject to the caprice of inexperienced young officers with higher rank, one being a colonel, a "simple teacher of natural and experimental philosophie," which was certainly the least necessary branch of military education "tho not altogether to be dispensed with." L'Enfant concluded the letter to Eustis by recurring to his federal city claim, which he did not question "the President and your self will consider the satisfaction of" to be "of as much interest to the reputation of the american name as it is of importance to me."[82]

James Monroe

James Monroe (1758–1831) was the last in a series of high government patrons to assist—or attempt to assist—L'Enfant. A former Continental Army officer and fellow member of The Society of the Cincinnati, Monroe had served as a U.S. Senator, ambassador to France, and governor of Virginia before becoming President James Madison's secretary of state, in which capacity he earnestly, but unavailingly, encouraged the aging and destitute L'Enfant to accept a professorship at West Point in 1812. The studio of James Sharples (1751–1811) produced this pastel on paper, probably while Monroe passed through Philadelphia on his return from France in 1797. (Courtesy of Independence National Historical Park, Philadelphia)

Madison and his secretary of war turned to L'Enfant's old friend Secretary of State James Monroe to persuade the engineer to change his mind. Before declining the professorship, L'Enfant had sought Monroe's advice that was, of course, to accept the job as it would provide an honorable place and salary and would not prevent him from proceeding on any claim against the government. Now Monroe wrote officially but "in the spirit & feelings of an old revolutionary fellow soldier & friend … without reserve." He knew his man and consequently took the claim head on. For two years as secretary of state he had done all he could to promote it, but in the process he had learned that some members thought Congress should not sanction it while others thought the amount requested too high. Monroe did not think L'Enfant would ever succeed, but "far from dissuading you, from pursuing it. I wish you on the contrary to do it, since you think the claim just & are much interested in it."

That out of the way, the secretary turned to West Point which he pictured as "a comfortable asylum and independence for life." There was no hope of something better; indeed "you are the only *foreigner* [emphasis mine] in the country for whom as much could have been done." The president had authority to allow its staff "to serve with the army instead of acting in the closet, especially when the army takes the field." Besides, the job put L'Enfant in a better position for pursuing his claim, because by serving the country again he would increase the value of his former services and bring them more into view as well as interest new and useful acquaintances in his welfare. It was a beginning and might lead to something better—"honorable ranks & pay, in advancing years, ought to be cherished." Monroe concluded by assuring his "old revolutionary friend" that he would never advise anyone to do a thing that was not "honorable and praiseworthy."[83] L'Enfant was not to be convinced and his only connection to the military academy is through his magnificent painting of West Point that the institution owns, rendered sometime after July 1781 when the British allowed him to leave South Carolina.

L'Enfant submitted his fourth petition in 1813.

L'Enfant had insisted in his letter to the secretary of war declining the position at West Point that he preferred hands-on to theoretical work. He soon got his wish. After the British burned Washington, Acting Secretary of War Monroe dispatched L'Enfant in September 1814 to reconstruct Fort Warburton (later renamed Fort Washington), just south of the seat of federal government and across the Potomac River from Mount Vernon. It was thus that L'Enfant came to spend most of the remainder of his life as the guest of a kind and fascinating man named Thomas Attwood Digges. The two had probably met in 1808 when both were residing at Rhodes Tavern.[84]

Thomas Digges descended from a wealthy influential Kent County English Catholic family. One ancestor had been active in the

Virginia Company and a long time member of Parliament while the immigrant ancestor had been governor of Virginia. Born in 1742 at Warburton, a Prince Georges County, Maryland, plantation, Thomas Digges may have gone to Oxford in the 1750s; if so, he may have pursued medical studies for he was known to some of his contemporaries as a doctor. Digges fled Maryland for Portugal in 1767 because of legal difficulties arising from "misdemeanours … indicating rooted depravity, but amazing address." Just what he had done is unknown, but it may have been related to his kleptomania. In Lisbon he became involved in the Portuguese international shipping community, claiming later that he knew personally every important merchant in the country. The handsome six foot-two Digges also became involved with a particularly charming "and remarkably beautiful" English woman whom he followed to London in 1774. But there were also allegations that he left because of renewed legal difficulties. The next year he published the rather autobiographical *Adventures of Alonso*, the first novel to be written by an American.

Digges quickly associated himself with the American community in London and with members of Parliament who supported the American cause. By the end of 1775, and for at least the next two years, he illegally engaged in shipping munitions to the United States; in the process he encouraged American sea captains and seamen in England to take themselves and their knowledge of the coasts of North America to France. His American friends in London included Ralph Izard and William and Arthur Lee, the latter of whom the Continental Congress sent to join Benjamin Franklin and Silas Deane as its representatives at Paris. In January 1778 William Lee recommended Digges to his brother, Congressman Richard Henry Lee, as a potential American agent in Portugal, describing him as a "sensible, spirited" man who "has been invariable [sic] employed in his country's services ever since the commencement of the dispute with G.B." Arthur Lee praised him to Samuel Adams. Consequently Digges became enmeshed in the trans Atlantic dispute between Arthur Lee and Silas Deane that rent both Congress and the American representatives at Paris in the middle of the War for Independence and that led to Lee's disgrace when Congress recalled him.

While Digges was clearly associated with the Lee faction, he attempted to win the favor of Franklin, a Deane ally. When Digges carried a peace proposal to Franklin from a pro-American member of Parliament in April 1779, Franklin administered the oath of allegiance to the United States to him. Digges returned to England where he assisted American prisoners in their efforts to escape and with money provided to him by Franklin, some of which he seems to have appropriated to his own use. "We have no name in our Language for such atrocious Wickedness," Franklin fumed; "if such a fellow is not damn'd it is not worth while to keep a Devil." Franklin's accusation against Digges did not include sus-

Fort Warburton
In 1814, Acting Secretary of War James Monroe offered L'Enfant one last gesture of official favor: the task of reconstructing Fort Warburton (now Fort Washington), the seat of government's last line of defense against enemy attacks from downriver. Part of his work appears in this later plan of the fort. But L'Enfant's final contribution to altering the Potomac's tidewater landscape was destined yet again to be cut short. Exhibiting the same independence for which he had become notorious, L'Enfant was relieved of the assignment at war's end. Although he continued to live nearby as the long-time guest of its neighboring planter, Thomas Attwood Digges, his host wrote that L'Enfant never after walked there or even looked in the direction of the fort. (Courtesy of the National Park Service)

picions of disloyalty, nevertheless, his reports about Digges earned the Marylander the enmity of several of his contemporaries as well as historians who have never evaluated Digges's career in terms of the so-called Lee–Deane Affair, the political litmus test of the Revolution.[85]

From 1780 to 1782 Digges worked closely with the American Commissioner John Adams, an ally of the Lees and no friend to Franklin, providing him with information and pamphlets about British politics— particularly the raging debate regarding the war—and news about Americans, such as Henry Laurens and John Trumbull, imprisoned in The Tower of London. Just as importantly, he made the arrangements by which Adams got his pro-American propaganda published in London. It was through Digges that British Prime Minister North sent peace feelers to Adams in February 1782, an activity that caused both contemporaries and historians under the influence of Franklin to misconclude that Digges was either a British spy or a double agent. The editor of Adams's papers calls the two-year, seventy-three letter correspondence—in which Digges used most of his more than twenty wartime aliases—"one of the most valuable" in the long political and diplomatic career of John Adams, or Ferdinando Ramon San as he was addressed by Digges.[86]

The best defense of Digges's Revolutionary War career came in 1794 when certain Marylanders attempted to use the state's confiscation law to prevent Digges from inheriting Warburton on the grounds that he had been disloyal during the Revolutionary War. His brother-in-law, Alexandria merchant John Fitzgerald, a former aide-de-camp to George Washington, a founder with Washington of the Potomac Navigation Company, and Washington's appointee as federal revenue collector at Alexandria, knew just what to do. Washington's character witness put the matter to rest, at least in the threatened legal proceedings if not in the minds of historians. Washington had "no hesitation in declaring that the conduct of Mr. Thomas Digges … has not been only friendly, but I might add zealous." Washington indicated that he had received useful verbal intelligence from his neighbor during the Revolutionary War carried to him by Americans who had escaped from prison in England and, if he recalled correctly, written ones as well. Further, the president noted, he had consulted John Trumbull, who informed him that Digges had assisted imprisoned Americans in England in escaping and who believed Franklin had employed him to do so. Trumbull had also heard, Washington noted, that a difference had arisen between Digges and Franklin over the settlement of their accounts.[87]

At the end of the Revolutionary War Digges described himself as having been exceedingly distressed for money since 1777 and at times "as much in want as any American prisoner I had the care of." By 1784 he had gone to Ireland where he encouraged immigration to the United States, particularly to Alexandria, Virginia, where laborers were needed by the Potomac Navigation Company. Digges's creditors caught up with him by 1785 and he spent at least a year in a miserable Dublin debtor's prison. There in his ample free time he authored at least one newspaper puff piece on the Potomac Navigation Company and a more serious effort entitled *A Representation of the State of Politics, Commerce, and Manufactures, in Ireland, in 1785, dedicated to the Congress of the United States of America, by a Citizen of Maryland*. That same year Benjamin Franklin returned to the United States. It was likely Digges who wrote Franklin's obituary for the *Belfast News–Letter* when he died in 1790. It was definitely John Adams, along with Senators Richard Henry Lee and Ralph Izard and their allies, who struck a blow for the by-then partially rehabilitated Arthur Lee by preventing the United States Senate from officially mourning Franklin's death.[88]

In 1788 Digges approached the new American Ambassador to France, Thomas Jefferson, for assistance with his activities in encouraging British artisans to immigrate to the United States, a logical outgrowth of his efforts in Ireland. He expected, but did not mention to Jefferson, that the encouragement of American manufacturing and free labor would hasten the demise of slavery in the United States. Jefferson rebuffed him on the grounds that government should neither encourage nor inhibit private business. Three years later, with active support from President Washington, Digges became an industrial spy for the United States, successfully providing the means for several English and Irish mechanics to immigrate with smuggled machinery plans and parts in violation of British law. In 1792, by which time he claimed to have sent eighteen or twenty such men to the United States, he had a printer strike off 1,000 copies of Alexander Hamilton's *Report on Manufactures*. These he distributed there, in Belfast, Ireland and in Liverpool, England.

Digges's most successful coup was probably William Pearce, who claimed that Samuel Arkwright ("then a mere hair dresser") had stolen his plans for water powered spinning machinery. Upon Pearce's arrival in the United States, Hamilton secured him a job with The Society for Establishing Useful Manufactures at Paterson, New Jersey. There he worked with L'Enfant who was impressed by the Englishman. Nevertheless, part of L'Enfant's troubles at Paterson arose from the fact that, as Peter Colt reported to Hamilton, "An *English manufacturer* cannot bring himself to believe that a *French Gentleman* can possibly know anything respecting manufactures."[89] In his 1794 testimony on behalf of Digges, Washington noted that "abundant evidence might be adduced of his activity and zeal (with considerable risque) in sending artizans and machines of public utility to this Country." In addition Washington mentioned that Digges had provided information to his administration a year earlier about the counterfeiting of American money in Great Britain. He probably also knew about Digges's interest in identifying British engravers for the United States's new mint.[90]

By early 1790 Digges had settled in Belfast where he became involved with the Irish independence movement and the founding of the United Irishmen. Insisting that the cause was doomed unless Irish Catholics and Protestants learned to work together, he joined the likes of Thomas Russell and Theobald Tone in discussing Thomas Paine's *Rights of Man*—"the Koran" of the movement. It was these efforts that led Catholic Bishop John Carroll of Baltimore to warn the Archbishop of Dublin about Digges's Maryland misdemeanors and unsavory Revolutionary War career in a letter that outdid Franklin in accusation if not in rhetoric. Digges's Irish years ended when, on a pleasure trip to Glasgow, Scotland, in July 1792, he was arrested for petty shoplifting. The police search of his trunks yielded items that he had purloined from his fellow tourists as well as friends in Belfast.

By 1793 Digges was back in London attempting to lay claim to his family's ancestral estate and forwarding American interests in conjunction with Thomas Pinckney and Rufus King, the American ambassadors. In 1795 another threat of imprisonment for debt prevented him from accompanying Pinckney, whose secretary he claimed to have been appointed, on the successful mission to Spain to obtain the treaty that would at last open the Mississippi River to American shipping. Digges had hoped to use the experience as a stepping stone to a consulship in Spain, or perhaps even the ambassadorship. In 1797 at Rufus King's request, he interrogated John D. Chisholme, an American adventurer who had come to London in an attempt to interest the British in a scheme to separate the Floridas and Louisiana from Spain. Ending what appears to have been more than a twenty year career as an American secret agent, Digges returned to Warburton at the end of 1798. A great patriot in Washington's eyes, Digges was a frequent dinner guest at Mount Vernon during the last year of his host's life. His ties to the great Federalist leader however did not prevent Digges from becoming a politically active Jeffersonian.[91]

Patient reader, do you remember Peter Charles L'Enfant, the man directed to oversee the reconstruction of Fort Warburton? Will you be surprised to learn that he did not last long on the job? It all began well enough, with acting Secretary of War James Monroe, Digges and L'Enfant strolling about Warburton discussing the possibilities and L'Enfant happily and ardently at work, even on Sundays. Trouble began after a few weeks when Monroe sent some suggestions to the engineer. L'Enfant fired off another one of his accusatory letters, chastising Monroe for interference. In May 1815 the engineer ignored a request from Monroe for a progress report until called to task by the chief clerk of the department. The report he belatedly submitted was an anguished defense of his work at Fort Warburton. Claiming that the criticism of his efforts had made him "pray for death," L'Enfant launched into the most excessive and vivid of his many self-pitying tirades. He was nothing more than a "naked cast away individual on a strange shore without home without friend without resources," a man "deprived of all relations on whom I could call for assistance and a debtor of several thousand dollars besides for the bitter bread I have [to] eat and this in a country too in whose cause I engaged in the early time of life [and] for whose service I bled and spent a good fortune." Monroe and President Madison took the easy way out of the situation—the chief clerk of the war department informed the engineer in September that the new peacetime military establishment act did not allow for his continued employment.[92]

L'Enfant had been living at Warburton as Digges's guest for one year. It was a match made in heaven—two old worldly Catholic bachelors who shared a house and meals in harmony, each pursuing his own claim against the federal government. Digges's claim sought compensation for a variety of alleged desecrations to his property since the building of the first Fort Warburton shortly before the War of 1812, and he lent this lobbying experience and his time to L'Enfant, assisting his guest with his claims against the federal government and New York City. The latter rejected a new petition in 1820, but Digges was informed privately that if L'Enfant was willing to settle for the $750 that had been offered in 1801 he could have it. Digges penned many colorful comments about L'Enfant and life at one hundred year old Warburton Mansion, which he described as often "nothing better than a hotel with me as the bar keeper of a tavern—all however pro bono" and so uninhabitable that his female relatives could not visit. (Other long-term guests included officers from the engineering department of the Army.)[93] We do not have L'Enfant's perspective on the friendship, but it is clear from what Digges wrote, and especially from what he did, that he had not only great respect for the "finished" and "able" engineer but also a deep affection that grew as the months passed.

Digges insightfully described L'Enfant to Archbishop Carroll, Digges's one time accuser, now a good friend and a relative by marriage, as "a faithful agent to his employers and an inflexibly honest upright man—slow & sure in his surveys but with too strong appetites to extend the works." L'Enfant's host recognized the effect that yet another professional failure had on the proud engineer and made no effort to encourage him to leave Warburton. In fact, he was careful not to give even a distant hint that L'Enfant's presence contributed to his own enslavement to the plantation. Digges had not been away from it since the British attack and he longed for a "quiet retreat" of one or two weeks in Washington. He could lock the house up to protect it from the untrustworthy young slaves and the thieving older ones he informed a correspondent, but how could he do that with "the old Major a seeming fixture here? For although himself temperate, quiet, worthy and ever orderly, my doors open to Him would become the Conductor to dinners, lounging night visitants, &ca., &ca. And You as a family man can guess the result." Having gotten the idea from L'Enfant that a position might be found for him in the war department, Digges immediately saw it as a way of *"escaping from home."* He recommended the engineer to the chief clerk of the department as "persevering, faithful to his employers, incorruptibly honest, and in no instance staining his hands with public money— a mere mite serving for all his personal outgoings and habiliments," and asked to be informed "as to the disposal of this good old Major (whom I would by no means injure)."

Thomas Attwood Digges

Thomas Attwood Digges (1742–1821) was L'Enfant's good friend and would prove to be his most generous protector. He supplied encouragement in L'Enfant's petition claims against New York City and the federal government, he lent a sympathetic ear (since he was pursuing his own claims at the same time), and he granted L'Enfant blessed asylum on his Maryland plantation, "Warburton Manor," where the "old Major" lived for ten of the last eleven years of his life. This portrait of Digges may be the one that family tradition attributes to Sir Joshua Reynolds (1723–92). A document among the family's papers indicates that the greatest portraitist in Georgian England did indeed paint Digges around 1775–81. But modern scientific analysis can neither confirm nor deny that this was the painting; the family lost custody of the work during the settlement of an estate in 1957 and its location is no longer known. The only reproduction is this photo, which appeared in the pages of the *Records* of the Columbia Historical Society in 1904. (Robert H. Elias and Eugene D. Finch, eds., *Letters of Thomas Attwood Digges (1742–1821)* [Columbia, S.C., 1982], pp. xviii, lxxii-lxxiii) (Courtesy of the Historical Society of Washington, D.C.)

In 1816 Digges was still trying to get to Washington for a few weeks "but my old Chum Major, the want of a housekeeper &ca. yet prevents me." "The old major is still an inmate with me, quiet, harmless and unoffending as usual," Digges informed James Monroe. "I fear from symptoms of broken shoes, rent pantaloons, out at the elbows etc. etc. etc. etc. that he is not well off—manifestly disturbed at his getting the go by, never facing toward the Fort, tho' frequently dipping into the eastern ravines and hills of the plantation—picking up fossils & periwinkles. Early to bed & rising—working hard with his instruments on paper 8 or ten hours every day as if to give full & complete surveys of his works &ca., but I neither ever see or know" his plans.[94]

Digges spent much if not all of the winter of 1817–1818 in Washington hotels. And, because of failing health and a severe hail storm that nearly ruined Warburton Mansion in May 1818, he stayed in town for the brief remainder of his life, communicating with L'Enfant by notes carried by a young slave. He apparently did not miss the house. "But for the old Major (a harmless honorable minded man & though a Great Oddity I believe as good an Engineer as any one we have)," Digges informed James Madison that summer, he would close the mansion and use the place only as a tobacco plantation until the completion of Fort Warburton, when the "ungovernable vile" soldiers reconstructing it, who robbed him not only of livestock but also of vegetables, were but memories.[95]

When the federal census taker came to Warburton in 1820, the "old major" enumerated himself as P. Charles L'Enfant, a white male American citizen over the age of 40, rather than as a foreign resident. The fact that rules and courts were not his favorite things and the absence of his name among individuals naturalized in Maryland and the District of Columbia between 1812, when Monroe referred to him as a foreigner, and 1820, suggest strongly that he never took the necessary legal steps to become what he considered himself to be.

L'Enfant continued to make trips into Washington to press his claim on Congress, asserting to a sympathetic attorney that he had evidence that the original federal city commissioners had made almost $100,000 from the sale of copies of his city plan in Holland alone. Newspaperman Benjamin Perley Poore left a colorful description of the elderly L'Enfant: a tall, thin man who wore a close fitting long blue military coat buttoned to the throat, with a high black neckcloth and no sign of a linen shirt; pomade-plastered hair close to his head, on which he wore a high bell-crowned beaver hat; in his right hand "he swung a formidable hickory cane with a large silver head" and under his left arm he often carried a roll of papers relating to his federal city claim.[96]

Thomas Attwood Digges died in 1821. L'Enfant remained at Warburton but his situation there quickly became tenuous and some-what unpleasant. William Dudley Digges wrote L'Enfant immediately after his uncle's death that he believed himself legally entitled to the property and enjoined L'Enfant not to give possession of it to anyone. But Thomas Digges's younger sister Elizabeth thought otherwise. Her opinion of L'Enfant must have been colored by the fact that she was the daughter-in-law of Daniel Carroll of Rock Creek, one of the federal city commissioners frustrated by the city planner in 1791. She won possession of Warburton in 1824. In February of that year, the same month that L'Enfant filed his final petition with Congress as the designer of Washington, William Dudley Digges invited L'Enfant to reside at Green Hill, his plantation adjacent to the District of Columbia in northern Prince Georges County, and to use the family's city house so that he could attend to his business at Congress with ease. Digges sent a wagon to Warburton for L'Enfant's papers and meager possessions. Despite his seventy years the old revolutionary soldier reached Green Hill on horseback. L'Enfant's new charitable protector went out of his way to tell his guest that his residence at Green Hill gave him great pleasure; the opinion of his wife, Eleanora Carroll Digges, the daughter of Daniel Carroll of Duddington, whose partially built house L'Enfant had pulled down the year she was born, is not recorded.[97]

"FEW MEN CAN AFFORD TO WAIT A HUNDRED YEARS TO BE REMEMBERED"

On 14 June 1825 L'Enfant died. He was buried in the unmarked slave portion of the family graveyard at Green Hill. Confusion about the name of the man who planned the City of Washington began immediately. The obituary called the "interesting but eccentric" deceased Pierre Charles L'Enfant, as did an early tourist guide to Washington published five years later. But he was Peter Charles L'Enfant in the legal notice filed by William Dudley Digges and printed in the same issue of the newspaper as the obituary. L'Enfant's estate was appraised at forty five dollars: thirty dollars for three gold and silver watches, ten dollars for a compass, two dollars for two pocket compasses, one dollar for "surveying instruments and books," and one dollar for "maps." His priceless papers, containing dozens of letters from several of the most politically important members of his generation were assigned no value. Digges preserved them carefully and while reading through them discovered that the lien that Robert Morris had placed on behalf of L'Enfant was worth $1,839.76, which he proceeded to collect. The sum was some compensation for a decade of a man's room and board. Another Digges family member was not so fortunate when, using the papers in 1849, he attempted to obtain compensation from New York City for Federal Hall.[98]

The federal establishment began to use the term "capital" rather than "seat of government" for Washington only after President Ulysses S. Grant made it a personal mission, and the Republican Party made it

public policy, to reconstruct the city both physically and symbolically. It was no longer to be Jefferson's federal town but the capital that Washington, L'Enfant and Walker envisioned. Newspapers and periodicals throughout the United States quickly took an interest in the city and all the new federal building construction projects there. In the process, a journalist discovered L'Enfant's papers at the Washington home of a Digges descendent. His article in the *American Architect* in 1881 was the first of several published over the next two decades to discuss "Pierre" Charles L'Enfant and his plan. While historians continued to refer to Peter Charles L'Enfant, the name that appears in the cartouche on his plan of the city, architects and others who wished to enhance the beauty of Washington apotheosized "Pierre" Charles L'Enfant. Congressional action reflected the debate over the name. He was Pierre in 1884 and 1895 when Congress considered an appropriation to build a memorial at his grave site. But in 1897 a bill was introduced in the House of Representatives to appropriate $50,000 for a monument to Peter within the boundaries of the city that he had planned a century earlier.[99]

The architects slowly prevailed however. Charles F. McKim, Daniel Burnham and Frederick Law Olmsted sold the idea of resurrecting the plan of "Pierre" Charles L'Enfant to Glenn Brown and the American Institute of Architects. In 1902 President Theodore Roosevelt and his cabinet went to William W. Corcoran's Gallery to look at the exhibit of models and plans mounted by the senatorially appointed McMillan Commission, which had concluded that the plan of "Pierre" Charles L'Enfant should be declared the basis of all future development in central Washington. But not only architects had their agendas.

Roosevelt, who was especially attracted to Roman Catholics and who detested the anti-Catholic nativist organizations protesting Eastern and Southern European immigration, was only too glad to give both the plan and the French Catholic "Pierre" Charles L'Enfant his blessing. Nor did it hurt that Roosevelt had become so close to French Ambassador Jules Jusserand that the president crowed that no foreign ambassador and a head of state had ever been so close in all of history. Within a year of his arrival in 1903 Jusserand had become concerned about German efforts to convince Americans that it had given just as much assistance during the Revolutionary War as France; in particular, he believed the Germans were trying to portray Steuben as a second Lafayette. For the French the apotheosis of L'Enfant could be very useful indeed and Jusserand did all that he could to support the cause.[100]

In 1908 Congress appropriated money for a grave site memorial to "Pierre" Charles L'Enfant. On the morning of 28 April 1909 his alleged bones, previously exhumed from Green Hill and taken to Mount Olivet Cemetery on the slope of Mount Hamilton in Washington, were ceremoniously escorted to the rotunda of the United States Capitol where

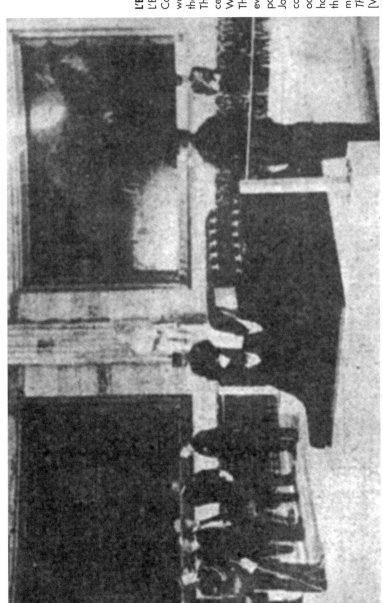

L'Enfant Lying in State

L'Enfant's lying in state in the Capitol rotunda on 28 April 1909 was a rare, and tardy, honor for the building's would-be architect. This grainy photo captured the ceremony for the pages of the Washington, D.C. *Evening Star*. The famous murals of landmark events from the Revolutionary War painted by L'Enfant's good friend, John Trumbull, look down upon the coffin. The event marks the only occasion in which an individual so honored had any living memory of the events those paintings commemorate. (H. Paul Caemmerer, *The Life of Pierre Charles L'Enfant* [Washington, D.C., 1950])

they lay in state on Abraham Lincoln's catafalque—an honor previously bestowed only on assassinated presidents and Radical Republican members of Congress. In the afternoon a military escort, followed by a mile long procession, conveyed the remains to Arlington Cemetery where they were reinterred with the best vista of Washington as a foreground.

Jules Jusserand delivered the major address, describing the American Continental Army officer as a "gifted, plucky, energetic but difficult to handle French Officer." Secretary of State Elihu Root gave the closing address: "Few men can afford to wait a hundred years to be remembered. It is not a change in L'Enfant that brings us here. It is we who have changed, who have just become able to appreciate his work. And our tribute to him should be to continue his work." Had L'Enfant himself been able to speak he could have done no better than to quote from one of his petitions dated almost exactly one hundred years earlier: "the work of a century will hardly now be sufficient to raise the city of Washington to that splendor and credit which twenty year[s] time may have gained to it, had its establishment been but only prosecuted … conformably to my sisteme and plan." The memorial itself, which included a marble bas-relief "blueprint" of the L'Enfant Plan, was dedicated on 22 May 1911.[101]

British Ambassador James Bryce, a political scientist, and William Howard Taft, recently defeated for reelection as president partly because of Roosevelt's third party campaign, insisted on calling the planner Peter Charles L'Enfant in *Washington, The Nation's Capital*, the book they authored for the National Geographic Society in 1913. It was a last hurrah. The same year, Ambassador Jusserand, an historian awarded an LL.D. from The George Washington University in 1921—the year he was elected president of the American Historical Association—published a Pulitzer prize winner entitled *With Americans of Past and Present Days*. It contained the first biography of "Pierre" Charles L'Enfant, the second Lafayette from France.

For a century biographers and historians have followed Jusserand and called the planner of Washington, D.C., "Pierre" Charles L'Enfant. It is time to recognize Peter Charles L'Enfant's full contribution to the early Republic and claim him as an American, just as we do Robert Morris, Alexander Hamilton, and the millions of other immigrants who followed in their footsteps.

L'Enfant's Grave Site

L'Enfant's permanent grave site lies on the slopes of "Arlington House," the plantation home built for George Washington Parke Custis, the step grandson of L'Enfant's most famous patron. The tomb—which includes a marble bas-relief "blueprint" of L'Enfant's plan for the city that lies beyond—remains as the culmination of the early Twentieth Century apotheosis of "Major Pierre Charles L'Enfant." (Photograph courtesy of William C. diGiacomantonio)

ENDNOTES

Digges	Robert H. Elias and Eugene D. Finch, eds., *Letters of Thomas Attwood Digges* (Columbia, S.C., 1982)
DLC	Manuscripts Division, Library of Congress, Washington, D.C.
DLM	Digges-L'Enfant-Morgan Papers, Library of Congress
DNA	National Archives, Washington, D.C.
PAH	Harold Syrett and Jacob E. Cooke, eds., *The Papers of Alexander Hamilton* (27 vols., New York, 1961–1987)
PCC	Papers of the Continental Congress, RG 360, National Archives
PGW (C)	W. W. Abbot, ed., *The Papers of George Washington, Confederation Series* (6 vols., 1992–1997)
PGW (P)	Dorothy Twohig, Mark A. Mastromarino, Jack D. Warren, Jr., eds., *The Papers of George Washington, Presidential Series* (10+ vols., Charlottesville, Va., 1987–)
PGW (R)	W. W. Abbot, ed., *The Papers of George Washington, Retirement Series* (4 vols., 1998–1999)
PMHB	*Pennsylvania Magazine of History and Biography*
PTJ	Julian P. Boyd, Charles T. Cullen, John Catanzariti, Barbara Oberg, Eugene R. Sheridan, eds., *The Papers of Thomas Jefferson* (27+ vols., Princeton, N. J., 1950–)
Steuben Papers	Edith von Zemenszky and Robert J. Schulmann, eds., The Papers of General Friedrich Wilhelm von Steuben, 1774–1794 (Microfilm Edition, Millwood, N. Y., 1984)

---

1. Brown to Jules Jusserand, 24 May 1911, DLM.

2. Kenneth R. Bowling and Helen E. Veit, eds., *Documentary History of the First Federal Congress* 9(Baltimore, 1988):36.

3. The first biography of L'Enfant appeared in Jules Jusserand, *With Americans of Past and Present Days* (New York, 1916); it is reprinted as the "Introduction" to Elizabeth S. Kite, *L'Enfant and Washington, 1791–1792* (Baltimore, 1929). The longest biography is H. Paul Caemmerer, *The Life of Pierre Charles L'Enfant* (Washington, 1950) but it must be used with caution. See also Fiske Kimball's sketch in *Dictionary of American Biography* (1932) and Pamela Scott's in *American National Biography* (1999). That L'Enfant studied architecture with his father comes from Moustier to Montmorin, 9 June 1789, Charlene Bangs Bickford, Kenneth R. Bowling, Helen E. Veit, and William C. diGiacomantonio, eds., *Documentary History of the First Federal Congress* (17+ vols., Baltimore, 1972–) 16(Baltimore, 2003).

4. The quotation is from what appears to be the last page of a petition to Congress; signed Peter Charles L'Enfant and dated [1801], it is in DLM. It also mentions "my long dependency on the honor, the justice, and the equity of the American nation."

5. DuCoudray to Congress, July 1777, Item 156:642, PCC; John McAuley Palmer, *General Von Steuben* (Port Washington, N.Y., 1937) 92, 100, 119, 126, 136; James L. Whitehead, "The Autobiography of Peter Stephen DuPonceau," *PMHB* 63(1939): 201; Washington to Lafayette, 25 September 1778, John C. Fitzpatrick, *The Writings of George Washington* (39 vols., Washington, 1931–44) 12:501.

6. "DuPonceau Autobiography," *PMHB* 63(1939):210, 215; Worthington C. Ford and Gaillard Hunt, eds., *Journals of the Continental Congress* (34 vols., Washington, 1904–37) 13:459; L'Enfant to Steuben, 24 May, 6 July, 8 August, 24 December 1779, Steuben Papers; L'Enfant Military Record, French War Office, Hugh Taggart Papers, DLC.

7. I am indebted to Pamela Scott for her thoughts about L'Enfant's use of pain relievers and the nature of his imprisonment. Philip Ogilvie pointed out to me that L'Enfant's father signed his paintings without an apostrophe; see also the photocopied Minutes of the Royal Academy, National Gallery, Washington, D.C., where he occasionally used an apostrophe.

8. Parole and Exchange Records, DLM; L'Enfant to Washington, 18 February 1782, Washington Papers, DLC; Washington to L'Enfant, 4 March 1782, Fitzpatrick, *Washington*, 24:43.

9. LaLuzerne to Washington, 22 April 1782, Washington Papers, DLC; Washington to LaLuzerne, 27 April 1782, Fitzpatrick, *Washington*, 24:174; Benjamin Rush to Elizabeth Graeme Ferguson(?), 16 July 1782, Lyman C. Butterfield, ed., *Letters of Benjamin Rush* (2 vols., Princeton, N.J., 1951) 1:278–82; Ford and Hunt, *Journals*, 24:324; *Freeman's Journal* (Philadelphia) 17, 31 July 1782; *Independent Gazetteer* (Philadelphia) 20 July 1782; LaLuzerne to Vergennes, 23, 25 July 1782, Correspondance Politique, Etats-unis, Foreign Copying Project: France, DLC.

10. Ellen McCallister Clark, "The Diploma of the Society of the Cincinnati," *Cincinnati Fourteen, Newsletter of the Society of the Cincinnati*, 37(2000):8–14; L'Enfant to Steuben, 10 June 1783, Knox to George Washington, 6 October 1783, Manuscript Records, Society of the Cincinnati, Washington, D.C.

11. E. James Ferguson, Elizabeth M. Nuxoll, Mary Gallagher, John Catanzariti, and Nelson S. Dearmont, eds., *The Papers of Robert Morris* (9 vols., Pittsburgh, 1973–99) 4:522, 8:255, 280, 704, 743.

12. Receipt signed Peter Charles L'Enfant, 15 October 1783, Manuscript Records, Society of the Cincinnati, Washington, D.C.; Washington to Knox, 16 October 1783, Washington to L'Enfant, 30 October 1783, Fitzpatrick, *Washington*, 27: 197–98, 213–14; *PGW (R)* 2:507n.

13. Charlotte Lenfant to Benjamin Franklin, 15 April 1778, William B. Willcox, Barbara Oberg, Ellen R. Cohn, Jonathan R. Dull, Dorothy W. Bridgewater, Douglas M. Arnold, Catherine M. Prelinger, Karen Duval, Claude A. Lopez, eds., *The Papers of Benjamin Franklin* (36+ vols., 1959–) 26:144; *Royal Gazette* (New York) 3, 10 June 1778; L'Enfant to Washington, 4 September 1778, Washington Papers, DLC; L'Enfant to Charlotte and Pierre Lenfant, 10 September 1787, printed in Caemmerer, *L'Enfant*, 422–23; Kite, *L'Enfant*, 7n12; Washington to L'Enfant, 28 April 1788, *PGW(C)* 6:213n; L'Enfant to Charlotte Lenfant, 26 April 1788, John D. Batchelder Autograph Collection, DLC; Destouches to L'Enfant, 15 September 1805, Mallet Roland to L'Enfant, 5 May 1806, DLM.

14. L'Enfant Petition, 1 December 1786, L'Enfant to Washington, 25 December 1783, L'Enfant to Steuben, 25 December 1783, Manuscript Records, Society of the Cincinnati, Washington, D.C.; Matthew Ridley to Robert Morris, 24 February 1784, *Morris Papers*, 9:131; L'Enfant to Hamilton, 29 April 1784, Manuscript Records, Society of the Cincinnati, Washington, D.C.; L'Enfant to Washington, 15 April 1788, *PGW(C)* 6:211–13. Washington continued to be involved with the issue of L'Enfant's French debts and the medals until 1788; Jefferson, until 1787. See also L'Enfant to Charlotte Lenfant, 26 April 1788, John D. Batchelder Autograph Collection, DLC.

15. Nuxoll, Gallagher, and Dearmont, eds., *Morris Papers*, 9:562; L'Enfant Memorial and Related Documents, 15 December 1784, Item 78, 14:595–605, PCC; Ford and Hunt, *Journals*, 28:16–18; L'Enfant to Henry Knox, 19 May 1784, 12 March 1785, Knox Papers, Gilder Lehrman Collection, Pierpont Morgan Library, New York; L'Enfant to Washington, 18 February 1782, Washington Papers, DLC. On the French engineering "system," see Antoine Picon, *French Architects and Engineers in the Age of Enlightenment* (translation of 1988 French edition, Cambridge, Eng., 1992), especially chapter 5.

16. L'Enfant to Charlotte Lenfant, 26 April 1788, John D. Batchelder Autograph Collection, DLC. The fact that L'Enfant spent most of his winters in New York comes not only from L'Enfant, "Richard Soderstrom in account with P. Charles L'Enfant," [post Dec. 1804], DLM, but also from his letters dated there.

17. L'Enfant to Charles Thomson, 7 November 1785, Item 78, 14:677, PCC; *Daily Advertiser* (New York), 22 November 1787, "A Traveler," *loc. cit.*, 23 November 1787; Vestry Resolution, 27 October 1788, I. N. Phelps Stokes *The Iconography of Manhattan Island, 1498–1909* (6 vols., New York, 1895–1928) 5:1222, 1233.

18. William A. Duer in his *New York As It Was, During the Latter Part of the Last Century* (New York, 1849) 16, and in an 1847 series of newspaper essays reprinted as *Reminiscences of an Old New Yorker* (New York, 1867) 44. The information is based on what he heard and saw as a boy. His father, William Duer, conceived the real estate development and organized the company. He was also involved in the Society for Establishing Useful Manufactures. William A. Duer later studied law under Peter Stephen DuPonceau in Philadelphia (Joseph Stancliffe Davis, *Essays in the Earlier History of American Corporations* [2 vols., New York, 1965] 1:332).

19. Petition to the Commissioners of the City of Washington, 30 August 1800, Caemmerer, *L'Enfant*, 381; L'Enfant, Undated Correspondence, DLM. Evidence for L'Enfant's role as an architect of houses is scant. In the first half of the twentieth century, Columbia University Professor William Hindley passionately advocated the "thesis that every large and handsome structure built in New York City between 1785 and 1810 not positively attributed to somebody else was a work of L'Enfant's." (Roger G. Kennedy, *Orders From France* [New York, 1989] 99). Among the houses named by Hindley were the original section of Gracie Mansion, the Duncan Phyfe House, the Jumal Mansion, and the Alexander Hamilton Mansion (Hindley Lecture Notes, Columbia University, New York City); Caemmerer, *L'Enfant*, 103–07, contains a lengthy list of houses supposedly designed and built by L'Enfant. The best study of New York at this time is Sidney I. Pomerantz, *New York, An American City, 1783–1803* (Port Washington, N.Y., 1938) 493.

20. William Temple Franklin to L'Enfant, 29 January 1787, Franklin Papers, American Philosophical Society, Philadelphia; Edward M. Riley, "The Independence Hall Group," *Transactions* of the American Philosophical Society 43(1980):7–42. Another hypothesis is that the New York "society"—though the precise sense in which L'Enfant used this word cannot be known—may have been the New York Society Library. Its books were dispersed during the Revolutionary War and it was not reconstituted until late 1788, soon after which it took a room on the third floor of Federal Hall. A trustee of the Society had run a newspaper advertisement for its missing books as early as February 1784 and, although there is no documentary evidence, it is possible that members were thinking about a building in which to house them. This hypothesis is strengthened by two facts: Franklin was at the time librarian for his grandfather Benjamin Franklin and the Library Company of Philadelphia was thinking about a new building. It held a competition and in October 1789 chose the design of William Thornton, the amateur architect who later designed the United States Capitol. Its new home was completed in 1790. (Charles E. Peterson, "Library Hall: Home of the Library Company of Philadelphia, 1790–1880," *Transactions* 43(1980):129–47.)

21. Richard Leffler, "The Grandest Procession," *Seaport: New York's History Magazine* 21(1987–88):28–31; Duer, *New York*, 23.

22. Frederick Augustus Muhlenberg to Benjamin Rush, 5 March 1789, Gratz Collection, Historical Society of Pennsylvania, Philadelphia; Robert to Mary Morris, 4 March 1789, Morris Papers, Henry E. Huntington Library, San Marino, Calif.; "Letter from a Southerner at New York," *Pennsylvania Journal* (Philadelphia), 18 February 1789; Maclay to Benjamin Rush, 19 March 1789, Rush Papers, DLC; [William Maclay], "To the Honorable and Right Honorable Members of the Congress of the United States of America, now convened at New—York," *Federal Gazette* (Philadelphia), 3 April 1789. For a detailed description of Federal Hall see Louis Torres, "Federal Hall Revisited," *Journal of the Society of Architectural Historians* 29(1970): 327–38. For Federal Hall's use by the First Federal Congress and its role as a patriotic icon see Bickford, Bowling, Veit, and diGiacomantonio, eds., *Documentary History of the First Federal Congress*, 12(Baltimore, 1994): xiii–xviii and 15(Baltimore, 2003) at 4 March 1789.

23. Steuben to North, 1 October 1788, Steuben Papers; "A Mechanic and Friend to Americans," *New-York Journal*, 26 March 1789; L'Enfant to John Adams, 17 January 1790, Adams Family Manuscript Trust, Massachusetts Historical Society, Boston.

24. *New-York Daily Gazette*, 1 May 1789; David Humphreys to L'Enfant, 11 June 1789, Tobias Lear to L'Enfant, n.d, DLM.

25. Ebenezer Hazard to [Matthew Carey], 12 March 1789, Marian Carson Collection, DLC; James Duane to L'Enfant, 13 October 1789, DLM; *New-York Packet*, 6 March 1789; "On the Federal Building," *Daily Advertiser* (New York), 19 March 1789; *New York Journal*, 1 April 1790.

26. Moustier to Montmorin, 9 June 1789, Bickford, Bowling, Veit, and diGiacomantonio, *First Federal Congress*, 16(Baltimore, 2003).

27. Pamela Scott, *Temple of Liberty* (New York, 1995) 16–18.

28. *Daily Advertiser* (New York), 3 July 1789; Philip Freneau, "Federal Hall" *loc. cit.*, 12 March 1790; "Crispin," *loc. cit.*, 21 August 1790. The cartoons appear as illustrations in Kenneth R. Bowling, *The Creation of Washington, D.C.: The Idea and Location of the American Capital* (Fairfax, Va., 1991).

29. *New-York Journal*, 10 March 1790; *Daily Advertiser* (New York) 24 March 1790; *New-York Daily Gazette*, 2 April 1790; Minutes of the Common Council, 1784–1831, 1:495, 536, 539, 542, 545, *Stokes, Iconography*, 5:1255–1267; Robert Benson to L'Enfant, 10 May 1790, DLM. The Council's resolution referred to "Pierre" Charles L'Enfant, one of only two times that I have seen it used during his life in the United States; the other was in 1820 when the Council used both Peter and Pierre.

30. For details of the fight over the location of the seat of federal government see Bowling, *Creation of Washington, D.C.*

31. *New-York Journal*, 15 June 1790; Thomas Fitzsimons to Miers Fisher, 16 July 1790, Fisher Family Papers, Historical Society of Pennsylvania, Philadelphia; Moustier to Montmorin, 9 June 1789, Bickford, Bowling, Veit, and diGiacomantonio, *First Congress*, 16(Baltimore, 2003).

32. L'Enfant Memorial, 15 December 1784, Item 78, 14:605, Committee Book, February 1785, Item 186, pp. 1, 3, PCC.

33. In one of his petitions to Congress, L'Enfant claimed that George Washington had asked him for a city and building plans well before the Residence Act passed Congress in July 1790; that in 1787 [1785?] he had made considerable progress in preparing a plan for surveying the site for a federal town on the Delaware River; that he had been advised confidentially to visit the different places proposed for the seat of government at various times and to report his opinion on them; and that he did all this at his own expense, making preparatory plans for various sites (Courtesy of Pamela Scott).

34. 11 September 1789, *PGW (P)* 4:15–17.

35. John Carroll and Mary Ashworth, *George Washington, First in Peace: Volume Seven of the Biography of Douglas Southall Freeman* (New York, 1957) 433; William C. diGiacomantonio, "All the President's Men: George Washington's Federal City Commissioners," *Washington History* 3 no. 1 (1991):52–75; Jefferson to the Commissioners, 29 January 1791, *PTJ* 19:68.

36. *Maryland Journal* (Baltimore), 18 March 1791; Kenneth R. Bowling, "The Other G. W.: George Walker and the Creation of the American Capital," *Washington History* 3 no. 2 (1991):4–22; L'Enfant, Undated Correspondence, DLM. It is Pamela Scott's considered conclusion that L'Enfant had a draft of his plan on paper for Washington when he arrived at Georgetown.

37. See William T. Partridge, "L'Enfant's Methods and Features of His Plan for the Federal City," *National Capital Park and Planning Commission: Reports and Plans, Washington Region* (Washington, 1930); John W. Reps, *Monumental Washington* (Princeton, N.J., 1967); Paul D. Spreiregen, ed., *On the Art of Designing Cities: Selected Essays of Elbert Peets* (Cambridge, Mass., 1968); Daniel Reiff, *Washington Architecture 1791–1861* (Washington, 1971); J. P. Dougherty, "Baroque and Picturesque Motifs in L'Enfant's Design for the Federal Capital," *American Quarterly* 26(1974):23–36; J. L. Sibley Jennings, Jr., "Artistry as Design, L'Enfant's Extraordinary City," *Quarterly Journal of the Library of Congress* 36(1979):225–78; Pamela Scott, "This Vast Empire: The Iconography of the Mall," in Richard Longstretch, *The Mall in Washington, 1791–1991* (Hanover, N.H., 1991); and Richard W. Stephenson, 'A Place Wholly New': Pierre Charles L'Enfant's Plan of the City of Washington* (Washington, 1993). On Hamilton's influence on the plan see the forthcoming work of Donald Hawkins.

38. Washington to Sarah Fairfax, 16 May 1798, *PGW (R)* 2:273; Bowling, *Creation of Washington, D.C.*, 106, 208–09.

39. William Loughton Smith, Journal, Massachusetts Historical Society *Proceedings* 51(1917):61–62; John Trumbull, Journal, *Records* of the Columbia Historical Society 2(1899):113; L'Enfant to Jefferson, 4 April 1791, *PTJ* 20:83–84; L'Enfant to Hamilton, 8 April 1791, Hamilton to L'Enfant, 24 May 1791, *PAH* 8:253–56, 355.

40. Lear to L'Enfant, 12 October 1791, L'Enfant to Lear, 19 October 1791, DLM.

41. Commissioners to L'Enfant, 9 September 1791, Item 23, Office of Public Buildings … of the National Capital, RG 42, DNA; "Amicus," *General Advertiser* (Philadelphia), 12 July 1791; *Washington Gazette*, 6-10 August 1796; A Spectator (George Walker) "Description of the City of Washington," *Maryland Journal* (Baltimore), 30 September 1791; *Gazette of the United States* (Philadelphia), 4 January 1792.

42. *PTJ* 22:89–91.

43. Many of the relevant documents are published in Kite, *L'Enfant*. Stuart to Washington, 26 February 1792, *PGW (P)* 9:596–602; Thomas Johnson to Thomas Jefferson, 29 February 1792, *PTJ* 23:164–67.

44. Washington to L'Enfant, 2, 13 December 1791, *PGW (P)* 9:244–45, 281–82.

45. Washington to Stuart, 20 November 1791, *PGW (P)* 9:209–13.

46. Viar and Jaudenes to Floridablanca, 26 March 1792, Foreign Copying Project: Spain, DLC; L'Enfant to Washington, 17 January 1792, *PGW (P)* 9:452–68; Jefferson to L'Enfant, 22 February 1792, L'Enfant to Jefferson, 26 February 1792, *PTJ* 23:141, 150–59.

47. L'Enfant to Lear, 17 February 1792, DLM; Jefferson to L'Enfant, 27 February 1792, *PTJ* 23:161; L'Enfant to Washington, 27 February 1792, Washington to Jefferson, 26, ca. 28 February 1792, Washington to L'Enfant, 28 February 1792, *PGW (P)* 9:594–95n, 603–06.

48. Johnson to Jefferson, 29 February 1792, *PTJ* 23:164–67.

49. Jefferson to Thomas Johnson, 8 March 1792, *PTJ* 23:236–37.

50. Proprietors to Walker, 9, 21 March 1792, Kite, *L'Enfant*, 168–69, 175–76; Walker to Jefferson, 9, 21 March 1792, Jefferson to Walker, 1, 14, 26 March 1792, Andrew Ellicott to Jefferson, *PTJ* 23:188, 244–45, 283, 322–23, 345–46, 368.

51. L'Enfant to Proprietors, 10 March 1792, Proprietors to L'Enfant, 21 March 1792, Uriah Forrest to L'Enfant, 21 March 1792, Kite, *L'Enfant*, 161–67, 177–79.

52. L'Enfant to Samuel Davidson, 13 January 1802, DLM; David Burnes to L'Enfant, 24 July 1794, DLM; John Trumbull to L'Enfant, 9 March 1795, John Trumbull to George Hadfield, 9 March 1794, Thornton to Roberdeau, 20 June 1795, Roberdeau to Thornton, 2 January 1796, C. M. Harris, ed., *Papers of William Thornton*, 1(Charlottesville, Va., 1995) 303n–304n, 318–19, 366–67n. DLM contains many letters to L'Enfant from Walker and Roberdeau.

53. Washington to William Thornton, 1 June 1799, *PGW (R)* 4:95; Andrew to Sarah Ellicott, 9 August 1791, Catherine V. C. Mathews, *Andrew Ellicott, His Life and Letters* (New York, 1908) 89–90 (the location of the manuscript of this and many other letters in the volume is unknown); Ellicott to Commissioners, 23 February 1792, Item 1, Office of Public Buildings … of the National Capital, RG 42, DNA; Silvio A. Bedini, "Andrew Ellicott, Surveyor of the Wilderness," *Surveying and Mapping* 36(1976):113–35.

54. Abraham Faw to Commissioner Daniel Carroll, 24 January 1792, Item 1, Office of Public Buildings … of the National Capital, RG 42, DNA; L'Enfant to Alexander J. Dallas, 24 October 1791, de Coppet Collection, Princeton University, Princeton, N.J.

55. L'Enfant to Hamilton, 21 August 1792, *PAH* 12:262–63; Roberdeau to L'Enfant, 21, 23 March, 18 June, 14 August, 8, 17 September 1792, DLM.

56. For a detailed history of the Society see Davis, *American Corporations*, 1:349–518. *National Gazette* (Philadelphia), 5 September 1792; Minutes of the Society for Establishing Useful Manufactures, 1 August 1792, Hamilton to Society for Establishing Useful Manufactures, 16 August 1792, L'Enfant to Hamilton, 21 August, 17 September 1792, Hamilton to James Watson, 9 October 1792, *PAH* 12:141, 217, 262–63, 388–89, 538–39.

57. Peter Colt to Hamilton, 28 February, 27 March, 7 May 1793, Nicholas Low to Hamilton, 4 March 1793, Elias Boudinot to Hamilton, 26 March 1793, L'Enfant to Hamilton, 26 March, 16 October 1793, Hamilton to L'Enfant, 29 March 1793, *PAH* 14:170–71, 189, 245–46, 253–54, 248–49, 258, 419–21, 15:363–65; Davis, *American Corporations*, 1:463, 466–67, 491.

58. Morris to L'Enfant, 9 May 1793, DLM; Morris to John Miller, 5 October 1797, Morris to L'Enfant, 24, 25 September, 19 December 1795, 15, 16 August 1796, Morris Papers, DLC; John C. Van Horne and Lee W. Formwalt, eds., *The Correspondence and Miscellaneous Papers of Benjamin Henry Latrobe* (3 vols., New Haven, Conn., 1984–88) 2:86; Frederick Wagener, *Robert Morris* (New York, 1976) 124.

59. Morris, Promissory Note, 22 October 1794, North American Land Company Stock, 20 February 1795, Morris to L'Enfant, 15 May, 20 July, 18 October 1797, William Rawle to L'Enfant, 13 January 1823, DLM.

60. Dorothy Twohig, ed., *The Journal of the Proceedings of the President, 1793–1797* (Charlottesville, Va., 1981) 296; Tench Coxe to Hamilton, 30 June 1794, *PAH* 16:539; L'Enfant to Knox, 2 July 1794, Tench Coxe to Knox, 9 July 1794, Knox Papers, Gilder Lehrman Collection, Pierpont Morgan Library, New York; Jacob Hiltzheimer to L'Enfant, 11 September 1794, DLM; L'Enfant to Hamilton, 15 September 1794, *American State Papers* (38 vols., Washington, 1832–61) *Military Affairs* 1:83.

61. L'Enfant, "Richard Soderstrom in account with P. Charles L'Enfant," [post Dec. 1804], DLM (This document contains a nine page defense against the suit that provides important biographical details about L'Enfant as well as information about his relationship with Soderstrom [hereafter Defense]); James Hardie, *The Philadelphia Directory* (Philadelphia, 1794); *loc. cit.* (Philadelphia, 1795).

62. *PAH* 3:430, 6:24, 16:318; Soderstrom, Passport, Item 167:379, Diplomatic Commission, Item 128:70, PCC; Charles Thomson to John Jay, 2 March 1785, Paul H. Smith and Ronald M. Gephart, eds., *Letters of Delegates to Congress* (26 vols., Washington, 1976–2000) 22:238–40n.

63. Sears and Smith to Congress, 23 February 1785, John Lowell to John Jay, 18 March 1785, William Tudor to Rufus King, 22 March 1785, Soderstrom to President of Congress, 21 March, 8 September 1785, Item 78, 13:603, 14:623, 21:353–59, 357, 375, 435, Edward Robbins to Rufus King, 7 April 1785, Item 41, 5:377–82, John Jay to John Lowell, 10 May 1785, Item 120, 1:254, James Bowdoin to President of Congress, 16 July 1785, Item 65, 2:257, John Jay, Report on Soderstrom's Conduct, Item 80, 1:89, PCC; Constable-Pierrepont Papers, New York Public Library, New York; Soderstrom to John Langdon, 6 August 1789, Langdon Papers, Portsmouth Atheneum, Portsmouth, N.H.; Smith and Gephart, *Letters of Delegates*, 22:632n-33n; Ford and Hunt, *Journals*, 19:702, 812–13; James Abeel to Sylvanus Bourne, 10 July 1790, Bourne Papers, Harvard University, Cambridge, Mass.; Defense, DLM. For an article on the incident see Gary D. Olson, "The Soderstrom Incident: A Reflection on Federal-State Relations Under the Articles of Confederation," *New-York Historical Society Quarterly* 55(1971):109–18.

64. Item 129:195, 198–274, PCC; Soderstrom to Jefferson, 16 November 1793, *PTJ* 27:389–90; Robert Morris to Soderstrom, 24 March, 28 April, 4 May 1795, Morris Papers, DLC; Defense, DLM.

65. Defense, DLM; L'Enfant to Hamilton, 1, 6 July 1798, Hamilton to L'Enfant, [3 July 1798], *PAH* 21:523–24, 527, 531–32; *PGW (R)* 3:360n. See Joanne B. Freeman, *Affairs of Honor, National Politics in the New Republic* (New Haven, Conn., 2001) Ch. 4.

66. Defense, Soderstrom to L'Enfant, 23 December 1800, DLM.

67. L'Enfant's petitions to the commissioners in 1800 and to Congress afterwards can be found in DLM, and at DNA, particularly among the Records of the House of Representatives (RG 233). A few of the earliest ones are printed as Appendix A in Caemmerer, *L'Enfant*, where the quotation appears at page 378. A careful comparison and analysis of them has yet to occur.

68. L'Enfant Petition, January 1801, DLC; L'Enfant to Jefferson, 3 November 1801, 12 March 1802, Jefferson to L'Enfant, 14 March 1802, Jefferson Papers, DLC.

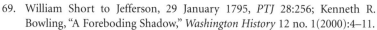

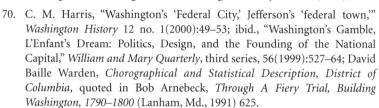

69. William Short to Jefferson, 29 January 1795, *PTJ* 28:256; Kenneth R. Bowling, "A Foreboding Shadow," *Washington History* 12 no. 1(2000):4–11.

70. C. M. Harris, "Washington's 'Federal City,' Jefferson's 'federal town,'" *Washington History* 12 no. 1(2000):49–53; ibid., "Washington's Gamble, L'Enfant's Dream: Politics, Design, and the Founding of the National Capital," *William and Mary Quarterly*, third series, 56(1999):527–64; David Baille Warden, *Chorographical and Statistical Description, District of Columbia*, quoted in Bob Arnebeck, *Through A Fiery Trial, Building Washington, 1790–1800* (Lanham, Md., 1991) 625.

71. Defense, Soderstrom Affidavit, 5 July 1804, L'Enfant to Mr. Brent, 14 October 1805, DLM; *National Intelligencer* (Washington), 20 August 1804; Ledger, 31 December 1803, Samuel Davidson Papers, DLC, as quoted by Arnebeck, *Fiery Trial*, 626; Van Horne and Formwald, *Miscellaneous Papers of Latrobe*, 2:230n; Kite, *L'Enfant*, 27; William W. Corcoran to Rep. John Kasson, 17 April 1884, Hugh Taggart Papers, DLC. For L'Enfant's legal problems see [John] Kearney v. L'Enfant, Chancery Records, Federal District Court for Washington County, Records of the District Courts of the United States, RG 21, DNA; Receipt for Settlement of Debt and Cost of William Worthington Suit, 9 January 1802 and John Davidson to L'Enfant, 8 March 1804, DLM; and note 73 below.

72. Robert Morris to L'Enfant, 14 January 1801, Thomas Morris to Robert Morris, 12, 20 January 1801, Robert Morris to L'Enfant, 22 January 1801, Thomas Morris to L'Enfant, 24, 29 January 1801, Elias Kane to Robert Morris, 31 January 1801, DLM; Minutes of the Common Council of New York City, 1784–1831, 2:701, 703–04, 709, Stokes, *Iconography*, 5:1382–83; L'Enfant to Hamilton, 4, 6 September 1801, *PAH* 25:408–10, 415.

73. L'Enfant to Knox, 12 August 1801, Knox to Dearborn, 16 December 1801, Knox Papers, Gilder Lehrman Collection, Pierpont Morgan Library, New York; L'Enfant to Dearborn, 7 May 1802, Dearborn to Mr. Simmons, 12 July 1805, DLM.

74. Morris to L'Enfant, 16 May 1802, L'Enfant to George Matthews, 1 September 1807, DLM; L'Enfant Obituary, *National Intelligencer* (Washington), 25 June 1825.

75. Statement of the Claim of Peter Charles L'Enfant, 5 May 1808, Item 46, Office of Public Buildings ... of the National Capital, RG 42, DNA; Victor Dupont to L'Enfant, 10 July 1807, DLM; Soderstrom, Dispatches, 1786–1813, Foreign Copying Project: Sweden, DLC; John Kantzou, Commission, 8 June 1815, Item 129:276, PCC. Only the administrative records, and none of the documents, survive from Soderstrom v. L'Enfant, Chancery Records, Federal District Court for Washington County, Records of the District Courts of the United States, RG 21, DNA; the only known document related to the case is Defense, DLM.

76. On Nourse and Delius see the Nourse Papers, University of Virginia. (I am indebted to C. M. Harris and Bruce Ragsdale for bringing the relationship to my attention.) On Decatur and Somers see Randy Shilts, *Conduct Unbecoming, Lesbians and Gays in the U.S. Military* (New York, 1993) 12–14. On Fulton and the Barlows see Cynthia Owen Philips, *Robert Fulton* (New York, 1955). On the changing nature of male friendship in the nineteenth century, see Jonathan Ned Katz, *Love Stories: Sex Between Men Before Homosexuality* (Chicago, 2001).

77. "DuPonceau Autobiography," *PMHB* 63(1939): 189–195, 214. On Armand-Tuffin and Schaffner see *PGW (P)* 3:41n. The post-War Washington-Lafayette correspondence, 1784–99, can be found in *PGW(C, P, R)*. The Laurens-Hamilton correspondence, 1779–82, is in *PAH* 2 and 3.

78. The best account of the relationship is Palmer, *Steuben*, passim. The Steuben Papers were sold at auction in 1929 and widely distributed. Thanks to the initial work of Palmer, the editors of the microfilm edition of Steuben's Papers located most of these letters and included them. Walker's letters to North do not survive in great number.

79. 12 June [1790], Steuben Papers.

80. 13 June 1790, Steuben Papers.

81. North to Walker, 30 May, 2 June 1788, 12 December, 4 October, 23 November 1789, Steuben to North, 18 September, 24 November, 12 December 1788, Steuben Papers.

82. William Eustis to L'Enfant, 7 July 1812, DLM; L'Enfant to Eustis, 17 July 1812, Item 2.1, Records of the Secretary of War, RG 107, DNA.

83. 17, 28 July 1812, DLM.

84. Monroe to L'Enfant, 8 September 1814, DLM. Except where noted information about Digges's life is from the lengthy biographical sketch that appears as "Introduction," *Digges*. For more on the controversy over Digges's loyalty see William Bell Clark, "In Defense of Thomas Digges," *PMHB* 76(1953):381–438; Lynn Hudson Parsons, "The Mysterious Mr. Digges," *William and Mary Quarterly*, third series, 22(1965):486–92; and Julian P. Boyd's unsympathetic assessment in *PTJ* 20:315n–20n .

85. Edith Ramsburgh, "*Sir Dudley Digges*," *Daughters of the American Revolution Magazine* 57(1923): 125–39; *Digges*, 467; Robert J. Taylor, Richard Alan Ryerson, Gregg L. Lint, Celeste Walker, Joanna M. Revelas, eds., *Papers of John Adams* (10+ vols., Cambridge, Mass., 1977–) 9:514–15; Clark, "Digges," *PMHB* 76(1953):383; Franklin to William Hodgson, 1 April 1781, Willcox, Oberg, Cohn, Lopez, Bridgewater, Arnold, Prelinger, and Duval, *Franklin Papers*, 34:507.

86. Taylor, Ryerson, Lint, Walker, and Revelas, *Adams Papers*, 7:214n, 9:ix (quoted) 11n.

87. Fitzgerald to Washington, 14 April 1794, Washington to Fitzgerald, 27 April 1794, *Digges*, lxvii–lxviii; *PGW (P)* 8:311n.

88. Bowling and Veit, *Documentary History of the First Federal Congress*, 9(Baltimore, 1988):242–43, 251, 252.

89. Digges to Hamilton, 6 April 1792, Digges to Jefferson, 12 May 1788, *Digges*, 408–09, 437; Jefferson to Digges, 19 June 1788, *PTJ* 13:260–61; *PTJ* 20:317n–322n; Carroll W. Pursell, Jr., "Thomas Digges and William Pearce: An Example of the Transit of Technology," *William and Mary Quarterly*, third series, 2(1964):551–60; L'Enfant to Hamilton, 17 September 1792, Peter Colt to Hamilton, 7 May 1793, *PAH* 12:388–89, 14:419–21.

90. *Digges*, lxviii, 441–56.

91. Parsons, "Digges," 488–90; *Digges*, 457–62, 467–68, 501, 504n. An 1815 letter to Bishop John Carroll indicates that Digges lost many of his possessions in 1798 when they went down with the ship transporting them to the United States (*Digges*, 575). Digges again undertook a mission for the United States in an attempt to head off war with England in 1812 (*Digges*, 532–39, 545).

92. James Monroe to L'Enfant, 25 November 1814, George Graham to L'Enfant, 12 June, 6 September, 12 December 1815, L'Enfant to Monroe, [post 12 June 1815], DLM; Digges to Monroe, 25 September 1814, 26 October 1816, *Digges*, 561, 586.

93. General Morton to Digges, 18 May 1820, DLM; Digges to George Graham, 22 December 1815, *Digges*, 572, 582–83.

94. Digges to Carroll, 18 August 1815, Digges to Graham 22 December 1815, 26 October 1816, Digges to Monroe, 26 October 1816, *Digges*, 582–83, 588–90.

95. Digges to Madison, 17 July 1818, L'Enfant to Digges, 25, 30 August 1820, 29 March 1821, *Digges*, 631–32, 636.

96. L'Enfant to William Bayley, 18 November 1823, Bayley to L'Enfant, 14 May 1823, 4 February 1824, DLM; *Records* of the Columbia Historical Society, 42–43(1940–41):107.

97. William Dudley Digges to L'Enfant, 24 December 1821, 4 February, 10 [16?] March 1824, DLM.

98. *National Intelligencer* (Washington), 25 June 1825; Jonathan Elliot, *Historical Sketches of the Ten Mile Square* (Washington, 1830); Appraisal of L'Enfant Estate, 1825, DLM; John Carroll Brent to J. B. Varnum, 12 October 1849, Varnum to Brent, 11[14] October 1849, DLM.

99. Kenneth R. Bowling, "From 'Federal Town' to 'National Capital': Ulysses S. Grant and the Reconstruction of Washington, D.C.," *Washington History* 14 no. 1(2002): 8–25; *American Architect* 10(1881):304. For historians' use of "Peter" see Thomas E. V. Smith, *The City of New York in ... 1789* (New York, 1889) and Bailey Myers, "A National Heirloom," *Magazine of American History* 10(1883):235–42.

100. Raymond A. Esthus, *Theodore Roosevelt and the International Rivalries* (Claremont, Calif., 1970) 15.

101. Caemmerer, *L'Enfant*, Ch. 10; L'Enfant to the Commissioners, 30 May 1780 [1800], *loc. cit.*, 410.

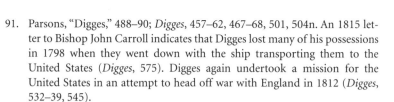